GRIEF EXPOSED

GRIEF EXPOSED

Giving a Voice to the Unspeakable

MIKE SOLLOM

WhiteFire
—PUBLISHING—

GRIEF EXPOSED: GIVING A VOICE TO THE UNSPEAKABLE

Copyright © 2022, Mike Sollom

ISBNs: 978-1-941720-83-7 (paperback)
978-1-941720-84-4 (ebook)

WhiteFire Publishing
13607 Bedford Rd NE
Cumberland, MD 21502

CONTENTS

Before You Begin

WHAT YOU ARE ABOUT TO READ IS AN HONEST description of what it was like for me to grieve. It's a personal confession of what deep loss can do to the human soul—what it did to my soul. It's not a prescription for how I think you should endure the grief and loss in your life. It's a description of how I'm trying to endure mine.

Everything was written in "real time" over the course of ten years. Whatever I was thinking at any given moment, I wrote down. I have not attempted to rearrange my writing into chronological order or reconstruct it according to themes or topics. I have flashed back and forth in time but done so without warning. I have, in fact, done very little to assist you or guide you as you read. I don't apologize for that. Grief and loss are not linear, nor do they adhere to logic. They are inconsistent, unpredictable, and messy.

The words that follow were not written to be read. I did not intend that anyone would see the squalls and scribbles that boiled up from the emptiness in my soul. As I sat in dimly lit booths in random coffee shops or wrestled through sleepless nights in my own home, my only intention was to rage against my loss and release the raw emotions of my grief.

In the end, I didn't write what might be true for everyone. I wrote what was true for me.

I began writing in a blog to inform loved ones of the ups and downs of my son Jim's battle against cancer.

Jim did not survive.

After he died, my words turned rough and raw, and I could not hide the honesty of my baffled and broken heart.

I stopped writing that blog, but I continued to write in a journal. What you hold in your hands are excerpts from that journal. It's what happened after Jim died. Those blog entries were the chronicles of a warrior son—my son. This journal is the journey of a wounded father—my journey.

THE WOUND
GOES DEEPER

IT HAS BEEN ONE MONTH SINCE MY SON WAS SEVERED
from my side. The wound is larger and more raw than ever. I
didn't know what to expect. I wondered if the "time-heals-all-
wounds" salve would soon be making its way to this gaping
hole in my heart. It is not. The wound is deeper now, more
vulnerable, and far more sensitive.

I used to tell Jim, and all my kids, when they started
a new job or a new class at school—filled with apprehen-
sion about all the unfamiliarity—to be patient. "Just wait a
month," I'd say. "It takes about a month and then everything
will start to feel familiar and comfortable."

This is not like that.

Nothing feels familiar or comfortable. My son is gone.
Jim is completely gone. There will never be a familiar or comfortable feeling with which to embrace this emptiness.

There is a permanence about this that—regardless how
hard I fight—engulfs me. Jim isn't going to come rumbling
into the driveway with the music in his Jeep pounding out its
familiar beat. He isn't going to come rambling into the room

with news of what he has just decided to do with the rest of his day. He isn't going to come ambling down the stairs, looking like he just stepped out of a fitness magazine, and greet me with that beautiful smile and his bright, "Hi, Dad."

My son is gone, and I cannot bear his absence.

DEEP VALLEY

SOMETHING IN THE HUMAN SPIRIT WONDERS HOW WE WILL respond to the pains and challenges of this life. We hear the stories and see the struggles of others and wonder how we will respond given the same circumstances and challenges. We put ourselves forward into the possible struggles ahead and wonder if we will rise to victory or fall in defeat. As athletes, we wonder if we can endure the exhaustion that finishing the race will require. As expectant mothers, we wonder if we will tolerate the pain of delivery. As soldiers, we question whether we will have the courage to stand and fight.

My confession is this: I haven't responded well.

I am the runner collapsed along the side of the road, too tired to go on. I am the expectant mother crying out for anything that will dull the pain. I am the soldier curled up in a foxhole, too frightened to open my eyes. I am frustrated, confused, and afraid. Anger, guilt, and shame consume me. I have not been like Job in the Bible who, upon losing everything, proclaimed, "Though He slay me, yet will I trust in Him." No, I am like Job's infamous wife who wanted to curse God and die.

I am not the prayer warrior leading my family in daily prayers of, "Not our will but Thine be done." My prayers feel weak and shallow and consist of sobbing and fist-shaking and, "Don't do this, don't do this. Please, God, don't do this. Please don't take my son from me." Even though he's already gone.

I long for comfort but all I feel is restlessness. The "peace that passes understanding," which I have promised to others in their deep valleys, seems to be passing me by. I ask for faith to bolster my courage and the courage of my family, but all I get is despair. I plead for protection but find myself prey to sin and temptation. I fast and wait on the Lord to renew my strength but I feel more and more exhausted every day. I ask God to reveal His Presence, but He disappears deeper into the shadows of this dark night.

I'M NOT FINE

I WISH THERE WAS A DIFFERENT GREETING THAN, "HOW are you?" I know that friends and acquaintances are concerned, but I wish there was another pleasantry to begin a conversation.

15

I know what they want to hear. They're hoping for an, "I'm fine," or "I'm okay," or even "I'm getting better." And, for the most part, that's what they get. But it's not true. My whole world has come to an end, so how could it be true?

The initial numbing shock is starting to fade and now the true pain of loss eats at my soul. Most of the time I can't catch my breath. My senses are dull, and my hands are unsteady. My heart beats so hard and fast in my chest, I fear it might burst. I wrack my brain in search of what more I could have done to help my dear boy. My mind wrestles to remember the simple sweetness of his perfect smile. I grope for a reason to get up in the morning and grasp for comfort to help me get through the night. There is an emptiness that refuses to be filled and a loneliness that will not be stilled.

I am broken. I am so badly broken.

I miss my son. I miss him so much. And, as yet, I cannot fathom how I will go on without him.

Untested Clichés

I HAVE BEEN THE RECIPIENT OF HARSH JUDGMENTS ABOUT my lack of faith. I have been chided for misunderstanding a "true" definition of biblical grief and loss. I suggested once that I would never see my son again. The reply was a bony theological finger shaking in my face. "Oh, Mike, you know better than that. You'll see him again in glory." I dared to express my anger at God for doing this to my son. Again, the chiding: "Oh, Mike, you know that's not true. God didn't do this, He simply allowed it." Perhaps the worst was my confession of deep grief over the loss of my precious boy. The reply: "Oh, Mike, you can't mean that. As Christians we don't grieve."

It's unthinkable that people believe they have the right to hurl their petty convictions at me in a time such as this. They desperately need to believe that their untested clichés are true and require my reinforcement of their suspicions. They are wrong.

I'm growing weary of the worn-out adage, "He's in a better place now." I want to believe that's true. I always used to believe. I used to recite the same sentiment to others. But it's different now. It's my boy that's out there—somewhere. Now I want to know for sure that it's true. I want to be positive he's okay. I don't want blind faith. I want sight. I want to see him running and jumping—a dream, a vision, anything. I want to know that heaven isn't just a story.

I want to know that my son isn't just *gone*.

TRYING TO COPE

IT'S UNSETTLING TO SEE HOW IMPATIENT, UNCOMFORTABLE, and intolerant some "friends" have become with my grieving. They seem intimidated and threatened by my outrage and my uncertainty. They have an inappropriate need for me to resolve my issues and find "closure." I'm being pressured to see doctors, consult with therapists, and turn to medications.

I'm not trying to get over the flu, beat some addiction, or improve my marriage. I'm trying to cope with the reality that I will never again be graced with the sweet presence of my firstborn son.

They want me to get used to this. I will never get used to this.

There is an emptiness in my life that nothing will ever fill. I have a Jimmy-shaped void in my heart that no one can ever replace.

IMPOSED PERSPECTIVE

I WILL LIVE AGAIN, I WILL LOVE AGAIN, AND I WILL PROBABLY laugh again, but I need to do that in my own time. There are some things that only I can do and there are some things that only I can say—things like, "I am so grateful I had Jim as my son for twenty-four wonderful years." Or, "What a blessing it was that my boy survived for eight months instead of the eight weeks the doctors had estimated." Or, "I'm not the first parent to lose a child and I won't be the last." Only I have the right to make those statements and only I will know when my heart is ready to make them. No one else, not even my beloved bride, has the right to impose that perspective upon me. No one—especially not the one who has never lost.

Those that impose—those who have—hurt me deeply.

I'm thankful for my fellow sufferers, those who have truly loved and truly lost. They aren't so foolish as to try to explain or rationalize. I'm grateful for my uneducated friends and for my non-Christian friends. They don't pretend to understand anything or attempt to say something "deep." They simply embrace me, declare how wrong this is, and assure me of their love. To you, my dear ones, I say thank you. Suffer with me a little longer. I need patience now, not preaching.

Stay with me.

THE SAME, ONLY DIFFERENT

AS MY WIFE AND I LEFT THE HOSPITAL THAT LAST NIGHT, I realized that nothing had changed. The receptionist was still sitting at her desk where she had been that whole week. The custodian in the hallway carried out his chores as scheduled. People moved to and fro as they went about their daily routines. Our van sat in the parking lot where we had left it. That familiar dent that helps us identify it from all the other vans was still there.

On the way home, it struck me how mundane and "everyday" life seemed. I saw construction workers finishing up their day, delivery trucks making their last deliveries, and scores of other vehicles sharing the road in monotonous sameness. I looked at the people in the cars as we sat at a stoplight. I assumed they were heading home at the end of their workday or perhaps on their way out for a nice dinner.

It was life as usual. Nothing had changed.

Except everything had changed.

The body of my handsome son lay lifeless and cold on that horrible bed in that awful room. I knew he was still there. The nurses said it would be another twenty minutes before they came to take him downstairs. Downstairs. To the morgue. The place where dead bodies go.

This is impossible. This can't have happened. How am I to bear this? I cannot. I simply cannot.

FUTILE HOPE

WHY IS EVERYONE TRYING TO ERASE MY SON?

Why must everything be canceled?

>His bank accounts—canceled.

>His university registration—canceled.

>His cell phone account—canceled.

>His Jeep registration—canceled.

>His health club membership—canceled.

>His credit card—canceled.

>His insurance—canceled.

Within days of Jim's passing,

death certificate after death certificate had to be mailed out

to document his death

so that his life could be . . .

canceled.

He was here. My son was here.

Jim had the fullest and richest of lives.

My heart and mind are still fighting so desperately

to hold on to the futile hope that

Jim has not really died
while the rest of the world
is demanding proof that he has.
How do I hold on to
memories of his life
when everyone insists upon
evidence of his death?

FULLY ALIVE

I REMEMBER MY SON AND HIS SPONTANEOUS AND unpredictable spirit. I remember his untamed heart and his romance with fantasy. He loved the unknown. I believe he had a love affair in his heart with the un-done, the un-tried, and even the un-thought-of. He would take off on his adventures without a moment's hesitation and with little to no preparation. With not enough money in his pockets and not enough fuel in his tank. With more confidence than common sense and more courage than reason.

I used to call it immaturity. He called it abandon. I used to call it foolhardy. He called it freedom.

If I am to learn anything from the life and death of my son (and I would trade a lifetime of learning just to have him back in my arms) then I long most to learn this:

Life is meant to be lived.

Jim was happier and more alive than most people. He lived his life to the hilt with complete abandon and a spirit of freedom. Jim lived his dreams. He lived every moment with his eyes and heart wide open. He didn't miss a thing. I want to be like that.

I want to be like my son.

HONORING GRIEF

THERE MIGHT BE A GLIMPSE OF WHAT LIES AHEAD IN MY grief. A change is coming. I entertain these thoughts not so much because I think I can get ready for this change but so that I might recognize it when it comes. There might be a line somewhere in my grief where I will either continue to honor my son or dishonor him. I think it looks something like this:

> I honor Jim now with my grief because he was so deeply loved and so dearly treasured. My grief over his death honors his life. My grief is a tribute to what will be missed by all who knew him and by all who never will. My grief honors what this world now lacks because he is absent from it.

I would dishonor my son now if I were to rush through my grief, diminish my grief, or even try to deny it. Celebrating Jim's life will be appropriate in its time but only in its time. Hurrying back to "business as usual" just to get my mind off things, rushing back to "normal" as if normal actually exists, and forcing the illusion called "closure" would be selfish acts aimed only at relieving my own pain. That would dishonor my son. My present pain is my truest expression of my love for my dear boy. Love is not truly understood without loss—without pain.

However, there will come a time, when all this pain will turn on me—when my grief will no longer honor my son.

There will come a time when my grief will begin to center on me, using my son's death as an excuse to feel sorry for myself and withdraw from life. There will come a time when I will use my sadness as an excuse not to be happy. A time when my loss will become an addiction, requiring more and more sympathy and pity to satisfy it and sustain it.

That will dishonor my son. And I must never allow that.

There is a line in there somewhere which I will cross that

will bring me from despair to hope—from sorrow to joy. A line that will change my loss back into life. There will come a time to honor Jim and celebrate the fullness of his life by celebrating the fullness of mine.

When this change in my grief happens—this crossing over from loss to life—I think it will happen gradually with many varying degrees of focus. I may not even know it's happening.

I don't know where or when this transition is going to happen. I don't know how to find it. I don't even know if I'm supposed to *try* to find it or just let it come. I do think, however, that it is coming. It must.

LOVE THE WORLD

JIM WAS A MAN OF FEW WORDS. WHEN HE SPOKE, HE spoke well. His words were thoughtful and well-chosen. In the last months and days, I listened carefully to every word. Those final days, as Jim struggled so desperately just to breathe, his words were limited and staggered. At one point, on that final day, with all of us huddled around his bed, he whispered, "I love you. I love you all. I love the world." His words rang with such divine familiarity.

All I could think of then was, "For God so loved the world that He gave His only begotten Son."

All I can do today is weep.

All I want to do tomorrow is follow in the footsteps of my son and "love the world."

ANGRY STILL

"DID YOU GET ANGRY?" THEY ASK ME.

"Yes, I got angry."

"Did you get angry at God?" they wonder.

"Yes, I got furious at God—furious at what He did and furious at what He didn't do."

Years ago, I read an article about a man who had drowned in a lake only yards away from the dock. The family of the deceased tried to sue a young man who was sunning himself on that dock, charging him with negligence because he made no attempt to save the drowning man. The family lost the suit. The courts determined that the young man had no legal obligation for the other man's life. It was, to most of the world, an outrage. It made people furious.

That's how I have felt toward God. He had no obligation to save Jim. Nothing bound Him to intervene. Yet, the negligence still torments me—the injustice still infuriates me. He could have saved him but chose not to. He chose not to. He *chose* not to. I hate that.

I'd rather believe that God *couldn't* save my son than that He *chose not to.*

I'm angry. Angry at sin. I'm angry at evil. At foolishness. I'm angry at complacency. And apathy. I'm angry at trivia. I'm angry at twisted priorities. (Oh, lest you misunderstand, I'm not just angry because I see these things in others. I'm angry because I see them in myself. I'm angry at the sin in my own life and the evil that lurks in my own heart.) I'm angry at the damnable disease that stole my son from me. I'm angry that I am forced to live the rest of my life without him.

Our lives weren't supposed to be like this. My family and I weren't supposed to suffer this wound and bear this scar. We're supposed to have four children. There's an empty chair at our table, an empty bed in our house, and an empty space in our hearts. Why wouldn't that make me angry?

Yes, I got angry. I'm angry still. I may always be.

DEATH CHANGES EVERYTHING

AFTER JIM'S DIAGNOSIS, WE FOUND OURSELVES IN A NEW world—the world of cancer patients and their families. They told us that our lives would be forever marked by Jim's disease. They said we would always count time as before his cancer and time after his cancer. I long now for that dividing line. That was like a crack in the sidewalk. This is like the Grand Canyon.

Death changes everything. The death of a child distorts every reality of a parent's life. LuAnn and I will never again experience a pure emotion. Joy will always have a cloud of sorrow. Pleasure will always bear a twinge of pain. Peace will always have that lurking presence of fear. Love will always have the reminder of loneliness. Faith will always have a shadow of doubt. In the back of our minds and in the depth of our hearts there will always be something missing, something out of place. Something will always be wrong.

Nothing will ever be the same.

PRETENDING

PEOPLE TELL ME I'M "DOING REAL GOOD." I'M NOT SURE exactly what that means. Maybe they say that because I don't break down and cry during every conversation anymore. Or it's because I can talk about Jim's life with a fairly steady voice. Maybe it's because I am walking through the "affairs" of the aftermath of his death with a business-like resolve. Whichever it is, I assure you it's all pretend. I'm not "doing real good" at all. Life goes on. Whether I'm "doing real good" or not has nothing to do with it.

I still cry many times every day. I still cry myself to sleep every night and wake up with tears every morning. The most bitter sorrow is in the middle of the night when all is dark and quiet and sleep escapes me. I am haunted by Jim's constant night-time struggle—his night-long coughing, his night-time sweats, his calling out for help, his pain, his vomiting, his impossible quest for comfort, his inability to sleep.

So, the nights when I can't sleep, I go to the couch where I used to sit and listen and wait for my son's call.

I sit and listen and wait but now it's quiet and dark—only empty silence.

I sit there now for hours, longing to hear his voice, longing to rush into his room—to help him, to see him, to touch him, to save him. I sit there now longing for God to hear *my* call—waiting for His response. I long for God, my Father, to rush into *my* room—to help *me*, to see *me*, to touch *me*, to save *me*. But all is quiet and dark—only empty silence.

So, every night I seek God in the silence. I seek Him with all my heart.

Come, Lord Jesus. Fill this empty place.
Mend this broken heart. Save this sinking soul.

LIKE BUILDING BLOCKS

THIS ISN'T JUST THE LOSS OF OUR DEAR BOY. THIS IS the disordering of all things.

There are six in our family. We have four children. LuAnn and I decided we would have four children when we first started dating at age fifteen. How can I say it any differently? What will I say the first time someone asks me how many children we have? Will I say we have four? Will I say we have four and just leave it with that or will I say we *had* four and try to explain? I don't know. No one has asked me yet.

How does this work? Is Annie the oldest sibling now? Is she expected to feel an added burden—an added responsibility? Jim, Annie, Nathan, and John were a perfect family. They loved each other. They *liked* each other. They truly enjoyed each other. They were like four perfect building blocks laid beautifully one upon another. What happens now that the first block has been pulled out? How do they restructure themselves? How do they reorder themselves?

I honestly don't know how it's supposed to work. We are six. Our kids are four—four, I tell you.

I am the father of four.

THE WORDS OF A CHAMPION

IT WAS UNBEARABLE TO WATCH HIM SUFFER. WORDS ARE too poor to communicate how terrible a sight it was—his young, strong, bright body gasping for air. There were long periods of time, especially at night, when everyone was asleep, that I would sit by his side and watch him. I sat in silence. I was aware of how easily I breathed—slow, steady, effortlessly. Aging, out of shape, pitifully overweight, I'm the one who should have been struggling to breathe, not him—not my boy. Even as he slept, sedated by drugs to ease his pain, calm his fears, and suppress his cough, his mighty chest heaved in a futile attempt to fill what was left of his lungs with air. Those of us who sat with him in the hospital that last week became nearly accustomed to that great effort—nearly.

When he was awake, he didn't speak of his struggle. He didn't complain. Even when the nurses asked how he was doing, his answer was always, "Pretty good, thank you." He took nothing for himself—no pity, no self-indulgence. Right up to the end, he seemed to have one particular goal: to protect us from his pain.

As the end grew closer, we all wept and struggled as we watched our valiant warrior fight for his life. At one point, I became overwhelmed by my son's battle. Without thinking, I took his face in my hands, looked straight into his eyes, and through my tears I cried out, "Jim, you don't have to keep fighting! You don't have to keep hanging on! You can let go if you want—let go of all the pain, let go of all the suffering. You can go to heaven. You can go to God. We'll be okay. We can let you go. But"—I held him closer—"if you want to keep fighting, then we are here for you. It's whatever you want. You decide."

By that time everyone had gathered around his bed. Weeping, we waited for his reply. He looked around at each of us and simply asked, "What do you all think?"

In unison the answer came back, "Whatever you want, Jim, whatever you want."

His next words will live mightily within me for the rest of my life. He pressed his hands against the bedrails and raised himself up. In a voice strong and steady, he declared with the resolve of a true champion, "I want to fight!"

Jim had decided and declared on Monday of that week that he would make it to Friday. We will never know what motivated that particular goal. His birthday was on the Thursday of that last week and I'd like to think his resolve was because he intended to celebrate his birthday with us on Thursday, but he wouldn't let himself die on that day. He had determined not to do that to us. As a result, his birthday will always be a celebration of his life not the commemoration of his death. His fighting spirit remains his final gift to us all.

Jim had declined any life support or resuscitation. This was *his* fight and *his alone*. He wanted no one else or no machine to fight for him. He would fight until he was done and when he was done, the battle would be over.

"I want to fight!" he said. And so he did. Death would have to wait.

WOULDN'T HE

TWO OF JIM'S BEST FRIENDS ARE IN FLORIDA OVER THE holidays. It's a special trip in memory of Jim to celebrate his life and to commemorate his love of the sand and the sea. I can just imagine that their conversations are punctuated with, "Wouldn't Jim love this?" "Wouldn't Jim love that?" And "Wouldn't Jim love to be here?"

At some time, our family hopes to return to California (Jim's true home) with that same spirit of commemoration. When we arrive at one of Jim's favorite places and smell one of Jim's favorite smells and see one of Jim's favorite sights, one of us is sure to say, "Wouldn't Jim love this?" "Wouldn't Jim love that?" And "Wouldn't Jim love to be here?"

It's Christmas. Jim loved Christmas. Our thoughts are filled with, "Wouldn't he love this? Wouldn't he love that?

Wouldn't he love to be here? Wouldn't he love the tree? Wouldn't he love the snow? Wouldn't he, wouldn't he, wouldn't he…?"

It's the "wouldn't he's" that make me long for the deep, unshakable sense of knowing that all is right—the surety that Jim truly is okay, and that heaven is everything and more than I could ever begin to imagine. If it's true, if any of it's true, then what he has now is so much greater and his love for what he has now and for what he's doing now is so much more sublime that he doesn't miss *this* at all.

It's *me* who misses *him* amidst all this. I'm crying for myself, not for him. The diminished life that I feel is in me, not in my son.

First Christmas

Our family traveled to LuAnn's and my childhood homes in Minnesota the Christmas after Jim died. Looking back now, I wish we hadn't. Our decision was based on our assumption that we couldn't endure a "family" Christmas in our own home without Jim. The problem with going to Minnesota was that Jim wasn't there either. In fact, he was less there than he would have been had we stayed in Michigan.

There was nothing in Minnesota to remind us of Jim.

There was nothing of his presence there. It was as if he had never existed. I wish we would have just stayed by ourselves.

The reality, most likely, is that no place on earth was capable of comforting us. Everything we did and everywhere we went felt wrong—felt empty. Jim was simply nowhere to be found.

WHY ARE YOU ALIVE?

I SEE YOUNG PEOPLE WALKING ABOUT—THOSE WHO would be my son's age—and I am angry.

> *Why are you alive? Why are you alive and*
> *my boy is not? What makes your life so special?*
> *What makes your life worth living?*

I wonder if they comprehend the value of their life. I feel anger when it appears they may not.

> *Do you even appreciate that you're alive?*
> *Are you living your life to the fullest? If you're*
> *wasting it then what gives you the right to live*
> *it?*
>
> *I resent you.*

Let my son live your life if you're just going to throw it away.

JUST THE BEGINNING

PEOPLE ASK ME HOW THE KIDS ARE DOING. THEY WONDER how the kids are coping with the loss of their big brother. When they ask that, I recall how I have coped with the losses in my own life. I remember how much I mourned the loss of my dad when I turned twenty-six. My dad had died when he was twenty-six, and when I hit that same age, everything took on new meaning. I remember how much I mourned his death when I got married and when I became a father.

How are the kids doing? They have only begun to mourn. There are many more tears ahead. I guarantee that the day after their twenty-fourth birthdays they will weep with the realization that, were they Jim, their life would be over. They will weep at their graduations, their weddings, the births of their children, and the for-no-apparent-reason days.

How are the kids doing? They're doing the same as their mom and me. We've only just begun to experience the absence of Jim in our lives.

How is LuAnn doing? Most of the time it's hard to tell.

She and Jim are so much alike—strong and silent, able to hold the pain inside, contain it somehow. She is coping with it in the deepest regions of her heart—her badly broken heart. Her firstborn child is gone. She suffers with an anguish that only a mother can know and only Jim's return could comfort.

HOLDING ON

IT'S BEEN ALMOST TWO MONTHS SINCE I LAST SAW MY son. With each passing day I miss him more. The emptiness grows and grows. It's impossible to comprehend that Jim is never coming home. Never.

Many fathers have had sons go away—off to school, or work, or the military. The missing grows, the loneliness grows, the longing grows, but those fathers know that one day their sons will come home. They mark that date on the calendar and count off the days. Even though the emptiness grows with every passing day, those fathers are comforted with the assurance of an upcoming reunion. It's that joyous hope that keeps them holding on.

What am I to do? Where is my assurance? My comfort? Where is my hope? What date can I mark on the calendar to keep me holding on?

REGRETS

IT'S THE FINALITY OF THIS THAT'S SO UNBEARABLE. My heart simply can't comprehend that Jim is gone—completely gone—that there isn't still some chance that this is all a dream and any day now he'll be coming home.

My mind wants to think, "He must be down in Florida again or off at school."

My heart wants to believe, "He'll be back."

He can't possibly be gone—not really, truly, forever gone.

What will I do? How can I go on without him? I don't want to go on without him. I don't want to go forward. I want to go back—back to when he was young—back to when all the kids were young and healthy and full of life. I want to "re-treasure" him. "Re-cherish" him. I want to reinvest my time, retract some of the things I said and did, relive the good times, rewind the bad times, and "re-do" them all.

I have many regrets. But do you want to know something wonderful? I don't think Jim does.

EVEN IF I COULD

I WANTED SO BADLY TO HELP JIM—TO DO SOMETHING, TO do anything. But he asked for so little.

One day I pressed him too hard. "What can I do for you, Jim? How can I help you?" In a frustrated tone, he replied, "What do you want me to say, Dad?"

Somewhat startled, I answered, "Anything, Jim, anything. I would do anything for you." My next statement was a mistake. I said, "I would take your cancer to myself if I could."

I had thought that many times. I had prayed for that. There had been many times, sitting with Jim as he slept, that I had laid my hand on his chest, closed my fist as if to clench those deadly tumors, and literally thrust them into my own body, pleading with God to let me bear his burden, begging to let me have his disease. This, however, was the first time I had spoken the words, "I would take your cancer to myself if I could."

Jim glared into my eyes and, in the one and only tone of anger I heard from him throughout the entire term of his struggle, he said, "Dad, don't ever say that again. I wouldn't let you even if you could."

I never said it again, but I never stopped praying for it. I never stopped hoping for it. I never stopped asking the heavens for that exchange. God didn't respond to that request. That would become yet another prayer that went unanswered. God didn't give me what I asked for. What God gave me was a beautiful, brave, unselfish son.

I DIDN'T SURVIVE

SOMEONE ASKED ME IF I SURVIVED THE HOLIDAYS. Obviously, they had some understanding that the holidays are particularly difficult for those who have lost loved ones. Perhaps they were even conscious of how terribly close my loss was to the holidays.

Did I "survive" the holidays? My response was not well thought through. I simply said, "Well, I'm here, I guess." Later, as I continued to rerun that question, that concept, and the word *survivor* through my mind, I realized, "No, I didn't survive the holidays." In fact, I haven't survived a thing. I don't expect that I will. This thing, this death, this destruction of my son, is not survivable.

They had the wording all wrong in the obituary—that terrible obituary, required by the funeral home and the local paper, that callously demanded immediate compliance and hasty planning. It said that Jim was "survived" by his parents,

Mike and LuAnn Sollom. We didn't "survive" his death. Surviving is when you come out on top at the end of an ordeal or when you make it safely through a difficult struggle. We had done none of that. We didn't survive anything.

The obituary should have read, "Those who are left behind yet to die." Or, "Those left behind *waiting to die—wanting to die.*" I don't want to be a survivor. I want to die and be with my son.

Parents like me who have lost a child don't only ask why our child had to die; we ask why we have to go on living.

THEY CALLED HIM SUPERMAN

NEAR THE END, REFERRING TO HIS CANCER, JIM MADE AN amazing statement, "I wouldn't trade this for anything." Incredible. How could he say that? He had to know his condition was worsening. He had to know his chance of survival was growing dim. Yet, as he observed the growth and change in his life, he had the strength of character not only to accept his disease, but to acknowledge some sense of gratitude for it. How did he do that? How did he find that light in the midst of his darkness? How did he find so much life in the midst of his dying?

Don't get me wrong, he didn't "embrace" his disease as some had suggested he should. No. He hated his cancer. He fought it with all his might. He didn't "embrace" his mortality. No. He despised death—that "final enemy." He wanted to live. Yet, in seeing God present in his life, he accepted and acknowledged something greater than anyone else could see.

All that at twenty-four years and a day—it's no wonder his closest friends called him Superman.

Jim's friends sat with him and watched old Superman episodes. Two of his closest friends tattooed the Superman logo on their backs in his memory. He became that for me too—Superman personified. I don't expect to meet his equal in this life.

As I ponder my astonishment at Jim's statement, a searing question penetrates my mind. Does he expect the same from me? Does my son want me to accept his death and to acknowledge some sense of gratitude for it?

I'm not ready for these thoughts.

How It Is
with God and Me

My son died. What difference does it make whose fault it was? My son suffered well beyond what I or most men could have endured and then he died. What difference does it make if it was according to God's "purposeful will" or His "permissive will"? What does it matter if God "fore-knew" it or "fore-ordained" it? What will change if I blame God's sovereignty or humankind's free will?

It doesn't really matter how I spin it theologically—God did it; or God didn't do it but He let it happen; maybe God planned it; or God didn't plan it but He knew about it—however I spin it, God had a hand in my son's death. I am so very angry with Him for that. I want to hate Him for that. I rant and rave and fuss and fume. I shake my fist in unbridled rage. I weep and wail at the loss of my son and do so, for the most part, without God's peace or consolation.

Not much fits anymore. God's power and my pain don't fit. God's love and my anger don't fit. Nothing fits. Maybe it's not supposed to. Maybe that's why I struggle so. I'm trying so hard to make everything fit and maybe it's not supposed to fit.

Maybe none of this works the way I thought it was supposed to. Maybe God is not who I always thought He was supposed to be. Maybe He is much more complicated—completely wild and untamable, utterly unpredictable and uncontrollable. Maybe it's God who doesn't fit—doesn't fit into the small places I used to keep Him.

Maybe modern theologians (and would-be, armchair theologians like me) are the greatest of fools. We sit behind our polished cherry-wood desks, pretending to understand who God is and who we are, audaciously determining which responsibilities, attributes, and duties are delegated to the Divine and which to the mortal. There was a time when I found theology both interesting and relevant. I have come to find it as neither. Theology is arrogant. Theology—the "study of God." How absurd.

It's wrong, this "problem-solving" approach to God—this "He-does-this-then-we-do-that" equation mentality—that has convinced us there could be some predictable sense of rhyme or reason to this mysterious Being.

My shelves bulge with book after book filled with feeble attempts to convict and convince a finite race about the concept of an infinite God. I'm so weary of words. I don't want to read another word. Words are weak. Words about God are useless, pitifully subjective, and maybe even wrong. I'm not entirely sure God wants to be figured out or even imagined.

Maybe He never intended to allow us such an impossibility. Maybe God wants something entirely different from us.

I'm not on speaking terms with God these days. At least not in those pompous meanderings I once called prayers. I was a good "pray-er." People always asked me to pray. I was articulate, theologically sound, and even poetical. However, the praying-est prayers I've ever prayed I prayed for my son, and they went unheeded. So, I don't pray like that anymore. Rather, I sit in silence. Maybe God can hear me better in silence. Maybe He can be known better in silence. So here I sit and here I think. Perhaps God is not who I always assumed He was?

Perhaps God is *not* mercy. If He was, He would always be merciful. Perhaps He's not grace. If He was, He would always be gracious. Perhaps He's not peace or comfort. If He was, these blessings would always abound. Surely He can show mercy, grace, and peace if He chooses to, but maybe that's not *who He is*. Maybe who and what He is, without measure or qualification, is Love—just love.

God is Love. I have seen Him *in* love. And, as anyone who is truly *in* love, I have seen Him broken, bruised, road weary, and weeping. I have seen Him tempted, hungry, and afraid. I have seen Him suffer and I have seen Him die. I have seen God in love with me when mercy, grace, and peace have failed. *I saw Him in love with my son.* I think God is love. And I think—no, I'm quite sure—that He is love, not just because He loves but because He bleeds.

Everlasting Tears

I STILL CRY EVERY DAY—MANY TIMES EVERY DAY. My tears are my constant companion. They pool behind my eyelids, waiting for the least reminder of my sweet boy—waiting, ready to erupt. They flow like a fountain in a futile attempt to wash away this pain.

I have cried every day for fifty-eight days. I cried that Saturday night when everything crumbled. I cried that Sunday night when Jim and I both knew the pneumonia was taking over what was left of his lungs. I cried the next morning when we checked into the emergency room. I cried every day of that last dreadful week and I have cried every day since.

I've cried for fifty-eight days. How much longer can it last? How many more tears can there be? It must come to an end sometime. I wonder, will I notice? Will I notice the first day I don't cry? I think I will and then—then, I think I will cry.

WHAT THE HEART SAYS

IN THE WAKE OF THIS CRUSHING WAVE OF GRIEF, MY LIFE has become numb and dull. A blanket of fog cloaks and covers. Life has lost its color. The vibrancy is gone. Details are blurred. Everything is muted. It's difficult to hear what anyone is saying. Or maybe I just don't want to hear. It's like watching a movie with the sound turned off.

People remind me, "Don't forget to take care of yourself. Eat and get some rest." I say thank you and tell them I will, but my heart says, "I don't care." A pile of pressing issues grows on my desk. Telephone calls remind me I must attend to this or to that. I thank them for the reminder, say I'm sorry, and tell them I will attend to this and that, but my heart says, "I don't care."

I am uninterested in the world around me. I just don't care anymore. I don't want to care. The worst of it is that I don't care that I don't want to care.

Once a soul loses something it cares about as much as a beloved child, the heart no longer wants to care about anything—ever. Perhaps it's because of the looming fear of losing again.

Nothing is safe now. If I don't care about anything or anybody then it won't hurt so much when I lose again.

I LEFT HIM

WHEN JIM PASSED, IT WAS SO SUDDEN IT SHOCKED ME. I thought I'd see it coming. I thought there would be more warning. Everything I had ever read or heard and everything the doctors had told me said he would wind down and wear out. He didn't. He fought hard right up to the end—to his final breath.

The instant he passed, I called for everyone to come to his side. Time and space ceased to exist as we held his body and wept. When I came to my senses, I asked everyone to leave the room. I called for a nurse. We released Jim from all the tubes and needles that had bound him. We removed his hospital gown, and I redressed him in the favorite and familiar T-shirt and sweatpants he had been wearing just four days earlier. I washed his face. I propped him up on the pillows. He looked so handsome. He looked so peaceful.

In turn I called friends and then family to his side. The hospital was so gracious. They gave us all the time we needed. That faithful, blessed fellowship of friends and family who had stood by him those final days and nights paid homage to their fallen comrade.

In the end it was just LuAnn, Annie, Nathan, John, and me. We all noticed how peaceful he seemed. How his face had changed as we lingered with him. His lips had pursed into a slight smile that was so natural to his demeanor. The kids took turns saying good-bye.

Annie commented on how good he smelled.

Finally, it was just LuAnn and me. We lay on either side of our precious son. We held him. Stroked him. We kissed him. We wept and wept and wept. Eventually, somehow, we knew it was time to go. I anointed him with oil. Then I drew the shape of a cross on his forehead, kissed that cross, and said a blessing—a ritual I had done with him since he was a baby. I covered him to his shoulders in a white blanket. As we prepared to leave, I caressed his foot and pledged my love to him one last time and said good night.

He looked the picture of health as he lay there in a peaceful sleep. He looked exactly the same as he always had, only he was entirely different. He was gone. And then…then, I did the impossible.

I turned, walked away, and left. I left my boy. My brave, sweet boy.

STAYING IN TOUCH WITH WHAT'S REAL

I'M OUT OF TOUCH. I HAVEN'T READ A NEWSPAPER IN over three months. I don't listen to the news or keep my eye on current events. I watch television. More in these past months than in the whole of my life. I watch but I don't see. I listen but I don't hear. It's only there to fill the empty space and dull the deafening silence. I've rented movies, but I fast forward through most of them. They hold no value to me. They're futile and foolish.

Will anything have worth again? Will everything be measured by the worth of my son? In his absence, will he become an "ideal" against which everything and everyone must compete?

> *Don't let Annie, Nathan, or John feel competition with the unreal and ideal perfection of their lost brother.*

How quickly we put our heroes on a pedestal and, in that perfect statue, forget their humanity.

I'm so absorbed in the loss of Jim, I'm losing touch with my other kids.

> *Oh, my dear ones, don't think Jim was perfect. He wasn't. Don't think that I loved him more. I didn't. I don't. I love you all the same—different somehow—but the same. It's just that he's the only one I've lost. He's the only one I have had to bury. He's the only one with a grave. My exalted admiration for him is because he's gone. He's gone and the only memories, frozen in my mind, are those of him at his very best. Annie, Nathan, John: I would be feeling exactly the same had it been one of you. You are all precious and all equal in my heart.*

Everything Is Lost

Okay, I give up. I quit. Game over. Stop the clock. I'm done.

> *God, whatever test You were putting me through, I failed. I failed. I confess. I failed.*
> *Now, call it off. Bring him back. All I want is my son back. I will live the rest of my life as*

the biggest failure and never ask anything for myself ever again. Just turn back the clock—bring us all back to the day before the world crumbled, back to the day before that MRI sealed his fate. Please bring him back. The loss is too much to bear. Please put everything back to the way it was.

God, You didn't just take my son, You took everything. What were You thinking? The black hole that has followed Jim's death continues to suck the life out of everything that ever seemed real. Wasn't the loss of my dear boy enough? I lost my son. Then I lost order, structure, balance, focus, clarity, confidence, composure, direction, stability, routine. I lost "normal."

I lost everything.

I have lost my will to live. God, when does the losing stop? You take away and take away and take away. Are You ever going to start giving back?

The human heart and the human mind—*my* heart and *my* mind—simply can't take in the enormity of this empty, bleak reality. My son is gone. My son is gone and he's not coming back. Perhaps *I'm* not coming back either. Cancer not only took my son's life, it took mine.

Dear God, what have You done?

BROKENNESS OF GOD

SOMETIME IN THE LAST MONTHS OF JIM'S STRUGGLE, desperate for a way to pray, LuAnn and I, in the depths of our brokenness, stepped out of our traditions to embrace the brokenness of God.

I purchased a crucifix.

It was made of walnut, about eight inches high, with a pewter figure of the crucified Christ. Every night we would hold it in our hands as we lay together in bed. We would hold it and plead for the life of our son. Some nights no words would form, and we just wept.

Holding the cross and the body of Christ created a new bond with God the Father because we also had a son who was broken and dying. Holding the cross and the body of Christ created a new bond with God the Son because He too knows how it feels to suffer and die. He knows pain. He knows disappointment. He knows anguish—and because He knows His own, He knows ours. In our struggle with our son's battle, we found solidarity with God and with His Son.

As we held the body of Christ, nailed to the cross, we felt His relentless love for us.

Just Getting His Stride

AMONGST JIM'S FEW BELONGINGS WAS A BIRTHDAY CARD I had given him one year and a day before his life ended. The card read, "Life is a trip, Son. Hope you always enjoy the ride…and you never forget the way home. I love you. Happy Birthday."

On the inside flap I had written:

> *I'm very proud of you, Jim…*
> *I believe you are on the verge of Great Things.*
> *It's exciting to see you finding your focus.*
> *Know that Mom and I are here for you.*
> *I am here for you.*
> *I love you!*
> *God bless you, Jim…*
> > *Love,*
> > *Dad*

He was just getting his stride. Just catching the wind. Things were starting to come together for him. He was finding his place in this world. He was growing up.

Jim had started truly confiding in me. He asked me questions, good questions. He wanted to know all the hows, whats, whens, wheres, and whys of life. We were becoming more like equals—two men talking about what it means to be a man, what it means to love a woman, what it means to serve God. He was just getting started.

Now that's all over. There are no more tomorrows for him. No more tomorrows for us. Our future has been taken away.

DADDY'S EMBRACE

HE TOOK HIM RIGHT OUT OF MY ARMS. GOD TOOK MY son right out of my arms. I wasn't strong enough to hold him, to keep him. I couldn't grasp him tight enough. I lost my grip. I lost my hold. God took him. He took him right out of my arms. All my strength failed me.

I'm strong. I've always been strong. But my strength did me no good. Nothing I tried worked. Nothing I did made any difference. I couldn't hold him. I couldn't keep him.

I want to see my son running free and fully alive. I want to remember him strong and full of life, but all I see is his struggle, his suffering, his pain. All I see is God wrenching him from my arms.

As I wrestle with these thoughts and images, I am reminded of holding Jim when he was a baby. Jim was born November 10, 1981. All our children were born in the eighties. The popular parenting tactics taught that if your baby cried after you laid them in their bed, you were to leave them alone and let them cry themselves to sleep. The "experts" claimed that if you responded to their cry, you were "coddling" them and spoiling them for the future.

Leave my children lying alone in the dark, crying and crying until they exhausted themselves? I didn't buy that.

When Jim cried, I went into his room, picked him up, and held him. Don't get me wrong. I didn't "coddle" him. I wasn't there to entertain him or let him "have his way." What I did was "contain" him until he fell asleep. Most of the time he kicked and squirmed and tried his best to break free, but I held him tight. In the end, just like the "experts" had said, he cried himself to sleep. The difference was that he cried himself to sleep in my arms. He didn't fall asleep alone in the dark. He fell asleep in his daddy's embrace. Then I kissed him, laid him in his bed, tucked his covers around him, blessed him, and left the room, knowing I would see him again in the morning. I knew morning would bring a new day.

I have always believed that the toughest "tough love" is the love that keeps holding on and stays in the fight, not the one that walks away.

Jim died November 11, 2005. He died in my arms. I held him tight until he fell asleep. The difference is that when I kissed him, laid him in his bed, tucked the covers around him, blessed him, and left the room, I knew I would never see him again. I knew morning would bring a new kind of night.

Longing for Presence

God, my courage is broken. My spirit is crushed.

> Where are You?
>
> Where is Your hand?

Christ, I am lost in this darkness. Only Your Presence can bring me salvation.

> Where are You?
>
> Where is Your light?

Spirit, I need You. I have needed You for so long.

> Where were You when I needed You most?
>
> Where were You when Jim needed You?

Jesus Christ, he wanted so badly to live. He fought for it with all his might.

> Where were You then?
>
> Why did You disappear into the darkness?

UNIMAGINABLE PAIN

I KNOW NOW THAT, EVEN IN MY MOST GENUINE ATTEMPTS to feel empathy with parents who have suffered the loss of a child, I have fallen painfully short of even imagining the anguish and agony the heart and soul and mind is required to endure.

It is relentless. It is merciless. It is unimaginable.

To those of you who have experienced my feeble attempts to empathize and understand, I offer my sincere apologies and plead your forgiveness.

I had no idea.

I had no idea.

THE VALUE OF LIFE

I SHOWED SOMEONE A PICTURE OF MY FOUR KIDS. Knowing of Jim's passing, he said, "At least you still have three left."

I wish people would think before they speak. Did this

person actually think his comment would comfort me? Was that supposed to be a consolation?

What was he thinking? Was he implying that my loss would have been even less significant if Jim had been one of ten children or even six? Would my grief be more justified if Jim was an only child but diminished somehow because he was one of four?

God, give me patience…

My Sensitivities Have Changed

IT WOULD APPALL YOU IF I WERE TO LIST THE ATROCITIES committed against my family and me in the aftermath of Jim's death. The "business-as-usual" mentality in which so much of our society functions has no time or place for matters of the heart—especially grief. This is truly a wicked world filled with cruelty and injustice. I am keenly aware of that now more than ever. I feel more offended by it.

Yet, the sense of goodness around me has also heightened. A part of me now dwells in the heaven of heavens. That reality draws the Presence of heaven near.

As a result, my sensitivities have changed—my sensitivities toward good and evil, my sensitivities toward people, my sensitivities toward society as a whole.

Shortly after Jim's death, unable to focus or function, I made a stupid mistake in my driving. No one got hurt, but a couple of people laid on their horns to express their disgust. The blaring sound and the anger of others were like daggers in my wounded heart. My anxiety rose so high, I thought I might explode right there in the intersection.

I vowed on that day, should I be imposed upon by someone's poor driving, that I will never be the one who honks.

I have no idea what might be going on in their lives. What if they had just lost their son? Their daughter, or spouse, or mother? What if they had just lost their job? We all live with pain. Many struggles in this life distract our focus and diminish our functions. I have no way of knowing what pain they may be, at that moment, struggling to endure.

Some drivers *are* idiots—talking on a cell phone or fussing about with a CD instead of watching the road. Maybe they deserve a good honk. But maybe not. I've decided it's not worth the risk.

I won't be the one who honks.

Living Without Balance

It's my equilibrium that's shot. It's this issue of balance.

We were six. We fit. Six was such a perfect number—an even number, a nice round number. We sat three and three in the car. We sat two, two, and two in the van. At the amusement parks we all fit perfectly in all the rides.

We fit.

Now we are five, and nothing fits. The equations don't work out. The teams don't divide up equally. The sides aren't fair. The balance is gone.

Is imbalance inevitable? Of course it is. Kids grow up, go off to school, get married. One day, eventually, we would be five, then four, then three, and finally the "nest" would be empty and LuAnn and I would adjust. Those changes are normal. Those partings are natural.

But this, this isn't a change. This is not a relocation. This is an *amputation*, and it's entirely un-natural—"un-normal."

So Depressed

I DON'T WANT TO DO ANYTHING, GO ANYWHERE, OR SEE anyone. I don't want to be anyone anymore. There is nothing that brings me joy, nothing that gives satisfaction, nothing that provides affirmation, nothing that offers acceptance.

I can sit for hours and do absolutely nothing. In fact, I do—I sit and do absolutely nothing. I stare at nothing and think about nothing. I don't move. I'm miserable and cumbersome. I'm more than a hundred pounds overweight. My knees are shot. I have constant pain in my back, knees, shoulders, elbows, and wrists thanks to arthritis, bursitis, tendinitis, and carpal tunnel. I have a pinched nerve in my back that leaves my left side numb if I lie wrong or sit wrong. I've aged twenty years in the last two. I'm old. I'm tired. I'm worthless. I'm a has-been. I'm a joke.

I have failed at everything I have ever tried. I have failed to guide my children, care for my bride, find employment, or stay fit. I have failed to love God. And then, I have failed to be strong in the face of all my failures. I have even failed to *appear* strong. I don't fool anyone anymore.

I use a strong medication to sleep. I use another to ward off panic attacks. I go through several different pills every day to relieve my anxiety and lift my depression. I take too many tablets of one painkiller every night to ease my body aches and too many of a different pill every day for my routine headaches. Then I must take more medication so all that crap doesn't come up as acid reflux.

I never used to watch television. For nearly two decades, LuAnn and I didn't even own a television. That was then, this is now. Now I watch all the time. I rent movies and watch TV. It keeps me from having to think. All I do is think—think, think, think—all day and too often, all night. Sometimes I think about how much I need to stop thinking.

I love my children, but there is a cloud that holds back pure joy. They remind me of such deep sorrow. Their presence amplifies "the absence." They struggle with their own loss and sorrow in ways they can't fully understand. They are all so stuck and don't see beyond today. They can't seem to find the courage or energy to move forward. From the outside, they seem to have no ambition, no ideas, and no purpose. When they lost their big brother, it was like they lost their place, their way, their footing. Their identity.

I know all of that isn't entirely true. My children are bright and creative. They've always had a good sense of themselves. They'll get it together. They'll get through this. It's just that there is so much potential and opportunity out there for them and I fear they just can't see that. Not yet.

I love my wife, but she often seems lost to me. I see her and I want her so badly, but she is so overwhelmed with sadness and despair that she cannot see me. She is fraught with deep fears of the future, burdened with providing for our family, and weary. Oh, so weary. She is tired of striving and sick of trying.

I truly love her, but she is not herself. She is not the woman I married. With the death of her firstborn son, she has lost her desire to love. I fear, like me, she has lost her will to live.

Who We Used To Be

LuAnn and I have become like porcupines. Every time we attempt to draw close to each other, to comfort or console, the razor-sharp prongs of our private pain inflict more injury.

There is a universality in our pain that connects us with everyone who has experienced the loss or absence of a loved one. Yet there is a uniqueness to our pain that singles us out from the rest, that separates us from other parents who have lost their children, and ultimately, that divides us even from each other.

We suffer together, yet we suffer alone. We lost the same child, yet our sense of loss is different. The same road brought us into this place of pain, but different roads will lead us out.

LuAnn and I are not the same as we were. We are different from before. We have gone astray in the fog—lost in a dreadful dream, caught between sleeping and waking. We desperately need each other but the "each other" we need isn't there anymore. We've changed. The death of our precious Jim has altered us. We're not the people we were.

What we really need is to be who we used to be, but there's no going back to that now. There's no coming back from this.

What we really need is for none of this to have ever come to us.

Wrestling with Prayer and Healing

One morning, on the way to a ten-hour chemo treatment, Jim declared, "I wish people would stop saying they're praying for me."

His declaration took me by surprise. I asked him why he would say such a thing. His answer was typical—honest and straight to the point. "Because I know they're not," he replied. I wanted to counter his comment but knew I couldn't do so completely. Not all those who say they'll pray actually do. Most of those who say they'll pray *every day* don't. It's merely an expression of concern, not a commitment.

Saying, "I'll pray for you," is like saying, "I'll call you."

Our intentions are good in the moment, but life proves to be too much of a distraction.

Certainly this was not true of everyone. I was able to console Jim with the fact that some were true to their words. I listed family members and friends who not only prayed for him every day but prayed for him many times throughout the day. I assured him there were people who prayed for him—people, like his mom and me—whose first thought every morning and whose last thought every night was of him and the earnest plea for his life.

Many prayed. Reminders came in weekly of people across the country and around the world who prayed. We received reports of complete strangers and random small groups in obscure regions that were lifting Jim up in their prayers. One day, I received a telephone call from an influential Christian leader in Bangladesh. That very day, thirty-thousand believers in Bangladesh were praying for my son.

Many prayed. So, why didn't those prayers get answered? Why didn't *my* prayers get answered? Was I not persistent enough? Not specific enough? Did my prayers lack power? Did my heart lack faith? Did I miss something—some special form or style of prayer, some special word, or phrase, or clause, or equation? I prayed in Jesus's name. I prayed in the name of the Father and the Son and the Holy Spirit. I laid hands on my son. I anointed him with oil.

I pleaded for God to heal my son, but his condition grew worse. I asked for a miracle, but God refused me. I started to wonder why I ever bothered to pray. What good was prayer, if when I needed it most, it failed? What good was a life jacket that wouldn't inflate when the cord was pulled? God seemed unmoved and unaffected by my prayers. It appeared that either God couldn't help my son or He just didn't want to.

What did I miss? What did I do wrong? Isn't the bleeding heart of a father enough to restore the broken body of his son? What about the tears of a mother? Why couldn't they have counted for something? How about those thirty-thousand people in Bangladesh? What was that all about?

I wrestle still with prayer, with healing, with sovereignty. The Heart of God, though loving and kind, is a mystery too hard to bear.

In the end, my fervent prayers had proven one of two things. Either God is not the God who answers prayer, or I had no clue what to ask for. My petitions served little purpose. And why should they? With all those fathers in this world who pray for their sons and with all those sons who suffer, why should *my* prayer be answered, why should *my* son be spared? Mortality is a given condition of humanity. At some point, we will all die. Regardless of how fervent the prayers of family and friends, we will all die anyway.

Did I think God was obligated to hold back mortality because Jim was so young or because he was *mine*?

Suspended in Uncertainty

NOTHING CHALLENGES OUR CONFIDENCE OR QUESTIONS our beliefs more than waking up one morning to find ourselves face down on a rickety bridge suspended between the two shores of What Was and What Is Yet to Be.

We boasted with self-confidence on the near shore about the stability of the bridge and the wonders of the far shore. Upon reaching the far shore, we will no doubt testify, with great humility, not only of our own efforts but of something "other" that brought us safely across. But, hanging out there in the middle with only a deadly drop below is a different story.

Life, death, and resurrection are surely like this bridge. We speak with great authority and confidence of life after death, of eternal rest, of ultimate healing, and of "absent from the body" being equal to "present with God" from this side of the chasm. (It's frightening how things so obscure can be so easily believed when left untested.) Then, one day, we wake up with our face down on that bridge, staring into the abyss below. Suddenly the "other side" doesn't seem so certain—so attainable.

I woke up one morning on that rickety bridge with the nightmarish reality that my beloved son is also suspended somewhere in that obscurity. Suddenly, belief is not so easy. Mercy not so consoling. Hope not so certain. Faith is not so confident.

Well-meaning people tell me to take comfort in the strength and power of God, to find solace in His loving arms. How can a young man take comfort in the arms of a father who just beat him? How can a little girl find solace in the embrace of a daddy who just abused her? Faith turns to fear when the One who claims to cure your pain is also the One who caused it.

Earthly images and musical platitudes about "crossing over Jordan" no longer suffice. Jim's present reality is so entirely different than mine that I can't even come close to imagining it. How can I gain sure footing on a bridge that is so completely unfamiliar? How can I know for sure that my boy is okay—that he's safe, that he's whole, that he's at peace? The faith to stand firm is fragile and unsettling when neither foot is planted on either shore.

I have lost sight of the far shore. Some days I'm not sure it even exists.

THE TASK OF LIVING

ONE OF THE REASONS I LONGED FOR SO MANY YEARS to return to the Midwest was its rhythm. The sharp contrast in the four seasons gives the sense of breathing in and out. It's a therapeutic out-with-the-old and in-with-the-new. Out with the cold chill of winter, in with the fresh radiance of spring. Out with the fickle skies of spring, and in with the long warm days of summer. Out with the hot humid nights of summer, and in with the colorful palette of fall. Out with the bleak, leafless fall, and in with the pristine white of winter.

Breathing. Inhaling. Exhaling. And with it, the knowledge that nothing lasts forever. For those who live in tropical or Mediterranean climates, it's easy to believe that it really could be summer all year long—that the sun could always shine.

Anyone who followed the end of Jim's life saw that "breathing." In and out. In and out. He would breathe in new life and new vigor as each treatment held new hope of recovery. Then he'd release a heavy sigh as test results revealed the tumors' resistance and retaliation.

I held my breath in hopes of recovery, but as the months went by, the reality of inevitability grew. One season transitioned into another. I couldn't hold them back. Hope was waning. Eventually, I would have to exhale—to resolve myself to the winter winds and the cold, impending night.

I felt like I was quitting. Giving up. I felt like I was failing my son. I hated myself for that. I was riddled with guilt. Jim was fighting so valiantly, and I was giving up. Jim was so confident the summer sun would break through, and I was giving in to the cold of winter. I suddenly hated the Midwest. I wanted to go back to California where it "never rains" and where the sun "always shines."

There is only one certainty about life—it ends. It has its seasons. It has its days. But eventually night comes, winter comes. Life might have its twilight hours and its Indian summers but ultimately, mercilessly, it ends.

This is not the last pain I will bear. This is not the final loss. Others will die in my lifetime—many others. Parents, friends, maybe LuAnn. The question in life is certainly not *whether* we die. Maybe it's not even *how* we die, *when* we die, or *why* we die. Perhaps the question of life, and its only answer, is not whether or not we die but whether or not we truly live.

I must get back to the great task of living while there is still some daylight left.

Reopening the Wounds

It's February.

I've dreaded this month more than you could know.
It marks one year since this nightmare began.
Something as innocent as a calendar will
callously force me
    to remember and relive
        every heart-wrenching moment
           of this terrible year.
Time is supposed to heal wounds
not reopen them.

What I've Always Done

We have a family altar in our home. It's not subtle.
If you come to our house, you'll see it. It stands at a focal
point in our living room where many homes might have a
television. It's an antique writing table covered with a white
linen cloth embroidered by my great aunt. An oak cross

stands at the back of the altar, sided by two white candles in brass candle stands. Fronting the cross is a pottery chalice, a brass incense burner, and a vial of anointing oil. At the two opposite corners of the altar are a leather Bible and a prayer book. Directly under the altar is a miniature cedar chest I built for LuAnn when we were in high school. Atop the chest is a clay pot. The pot is broken.

There is a single drawer in the front of the altar. The drawer holds extra candles, incense, matches, communion ware, a sheer black cloth, and a brass figure of the crucified Christ wrapped carefully in a white linen cloth.

Every Ash Wednesday, I take the figure of Christ from the drawer and unwrap it. In a ceremonial and symbolic manner, I nail the body of Christ to the cross. It remains there, unapologetically, throughout the Season of Lent. On Good Friday, I drape the entire altar with the sheer black cloth. Early on Easter morning, I rise, take the black draping from the altar, remove the body of Christ from the cross, wrap it in the linen cloth, and lay them all back in the drawer. I place a lily across the altar and proclaim, "He is risen!" I awaken the family with, "He is risen!" (If they're coherent enough and can remember, they reply, "He is risen indeed!")

Today is Easter Sunday—Resurrection Sunday. I removed the black cloth, but I didn't remove the brass figure of the crucified Christ. I didn't wrap it in its linen cloth. I didn't place it back in the drawer. I didn't lay a lily across the altar, and I didn't proclaim that anyone had risen.

The altar is collecting dust. The candles haven't been lit.

The incense hasn't been burned, the oil hasn't been poured, the Bible hasn't been read, the prayers haven't been recited. But more than that—more than all that—the body of Christ hasn't come down from the cross. Humanity and brokenness still cling to the cross. Perhaps it's *my* humanity and *my* brokenness. The silence of this moment is deafening. The confusion I feel is overwhelming.

I wanted a resurrection miracle today. Was that too much to ask? Will that always be too much to ask?

All is silent now—silent and indifferent.

I didn't neglect the altar and our traditions out of intention or malice. I simply didn't do what I've always done. I rose early, went to the altar, and removed the black cloth. But that was all I could do. I simply couldn't do what I have always done.

A Promise Broken

OVER A YEAR AGO, I PROMISED MY DEAR BOY THAT I wouldn't cut my hair until he got better. I kept that promise until today. Today I cut my hair.

Jim had received a few radical chemo treatments and all his hair was gone. Two of his best friends shaved their heads in a generous act of support and challenged me to do the same. Having "come of age" in the sixties, it's more my inclination to grow hair than cut it so I told Jim, "I promise I won't cut my hair until you get better."

He didn't get better. He died.

That bothers some people's theology who chide me with pious notions of the afterlife: "But Mike, you know he *did* get better."

I bite my tongue but my heart screams out:

> *Don't say that. He didn't "get better." Don't ever say that again.*
>
> *You weren't there. You didn't watch him suffer. You didn't feel him die. You didn't hear his last gasp for air. You didn't see the color drain from his face. You didn't smell his bed sheets, sweat-drenched from his battle. You didn't taste his lips as you tried desperately to breathe your own life back into his exhausted body. You didn't cry out his name, pleading with him to wake up and assure you it was all an awful dream. You didn't cradle him as he succumbed to the cancer, his lungs so full of tumors that he literally suffocated in your arms. You didn't do that. You didn't do any of that.*
>
> *I did. I did all that. So don't tell me he got better.*

My son fought to live and then he died. He died and then I had to kiss him good-bye and leave him where he lay.

Tell me how much you loved him. Tell me how badly you

miss him. Tell me how terribly wrong all this is. Tell me how sorry you are he's gone. Tell me that you believe my brave boy will rise again to New Life. But please, don't tell me he "got better."

For over a year, as I promised, I didn't cut my hair.

Today, I cut my hair.

Today, I broke my promise.

Forgive me, Jim. I'm so, so sorry. I'm not leaving you behind. I'm just trying to move forward. I'm not forgetting you. I'm just trying to remember something other than your pain.

Afraid of Tomorrow

I'M SO BOUND UP IN THE TROUBLES OF TODAY, I DON'T want tomorrow to come. That's more than being anxious for tomorrow. That's being afraid of tomorrow.

After a year of having every new day bring more trouble than the day before, I've become gun-shy of even waking up in the morning. I used to sing the words of an old hymn, "Morning by morning new mercies I see." Either the author had received more grace than I have to see those mercies, or he made it all up. I would suspect humankind has tried tactics to make themselves feel better about the relentless dai-liness of their lives since the beginning of time.

There are moments when I would do anything to feel better, to feel less alone, to alter my mood, to dull my pain. I understand now where addictions come from, and I really don't want any more tomorrows.

> *The day after I wrote this—six months after Jim died—I got a call from my stepdad. Mom had taken a turn for the worse. I rushed to her side. She died shortly after midnight.*
>
> *Do you understand me now when I say I don't want any more tomorrows?*

I COULDN'T GRIEVE FOR BOTH

IF I FELT LOST BEFORE, THEN I DON'T KNOW WHAT TO CALL this. While in Minnesota, grieving the loss of my mom and trying to both give and receive comfort, it was like I'd stepped back in time. As if nothing else—nothing other than that time and place—was real. It was as if everything prior in my life was just a dream. Maybe it was God's grace allowing me to focus on my dad and my sisters. Maybe it was my psyche blocking out all other pain. Maybe the two are one and the same. Whatever it was, it felt like Jim's death never happened. I didn't like that. I felt awful. I felt guilty. It seemed like I was forgetting my son.

I had flown to Minnesota alone. LuAnn and the kids followed in the car to join me for the memorial and burial. The kids returned to Michigan on Amtrak the day after Mom's funeral and LuAnn and I drove the following week. It happened to be Mother's Day. It was a dark and lonely trip. We rode in sad silence—a mother weeping for her son and a son weeping for his mother.

I'm in Michigan now. It's like I've stepped back into another time and space. Jim's death feels so fresh again. It overwhelms me. From here and now, it seems like I'm forgetting my mom. I don't like that either.

I haven't forgotten you, Mom. I haven't forgotten you, Son. I just can't grieve for you both at the same time. My heart can't take it.

PRAYING PAIN

MY STEPDAD IS THE ONLY DAD I'VE EVER KNOWN. HE IS a wonderful man—a faithful and devoted Christian gentleman.

He buried his wife, my mom, on the first Saturday of May under the mid-afternoon Minnesota sun. The next morning, as was his habit, he and I were in Sunday school. As the class began, the teacher turned to Dad and asked him to open in prayer. I couldn't believe it. It was inappropriate. Didn't she realize what he had just been through? Couldn't *she* have prayed?

The next night, we went to a dinner meeting. They asked my grieving dad to pray for their meal. The following night we went to a friend's house for supper. Again, Dad was asked to pray. How could these people ask this poor man to pray on their behalf when they should be praying for him? It made me angry. Dad was gracious. He prayed. It brought him to tears every time, but he prayed.

People asked me to pray after Jim died too. I didn't want them to ask, but they did. I didn't want to pray but, like my dad, I did. I fumbled and mumbled my way through.

I'm a minister. I pray professionally. I've made my living out of praying. I can put together a good prayer like a toast-master puts together a good toast—a nice, proper, churchy, theologically-correct "toast" to make everybody feel whatever it is they're supposed to feel (or whatever I think they're supposed to feel). I've always been good at that kind of "performance" praying. I probably still am.

Someone actually asked me what it's like to pray after suffering such a great loss? It's like this:

"Oh, God...Oh, God...Dear God!...
Sweet Jesus...OH, GOD!...Dear Jesus...Sweet
Jesus...Dear God Almighty..."

There. That's what it's like for me to pray. It's painful. I can't find the right words. I can't think of anything coherent to say. Nothing makes any sense. Nothing matters. What does anyone expect? I pray as best I can which is mostly that I can't. So, mostly, I don't.

No Logic To Explain

GRIEF COMES AND GOES AT ITS OWN DISCRETION. IT ebbs and flows with no discernible pattern. Sometimes it's like a leaky faucet, dripping with a relentless unsettling that never overwhelms you but never lets you rest. Sometimes it's like the whole ocean, crashing down with such a heaviness you feel you're being crushed.

I've read books and attended seminars about grief, the stages of grief, and instructions on how to lead people to the "other side" of grief. I've walked through and worked out the equations of what's supposed to happen first and second and so on—of the initial shock, then the denial, and of what to expect the first day, the first week, the first month, and the first year. There are even graphs, charts, and diagrams. The equations made sense. They seemed reasonable, even logical. I followed the format and faithfully guided mourners through their pain and loss. It all seemed so right.

It was all so wrong.

FEELING THE PAIN OF OTHERS

I STAYED WITH MY DAD FOR A COUPLE OF WEEKS AFTER my mom died. Dad had basically abandoned the farm for fourteen months to care for Mom. We had to clean things up, air things out, and get the old well up and running. As *was* his habit—*is* his habit still—we went to Sunday school, church, prayer meetings, and Bible studies during those weeks.

The Sunday school class was studying the book of James. I was glad. I love James. I opened my Bible to expose six completely devoured pages. As I scanned across the five familiar chapters, my eyes froze on my own handwriting at the bottom of the last page. I had written a prayer—a one-sentence prayer.

"LORD, let me feel the pain of others so I can pray as if it was mine."

It stunned me. My body went limp.

When had I written those words? What part of the text had prompted such a prayer? How could I have dared to pray such a thing? Why did I think it? Why did I want it? Why did I pray it? Why did I write it down? What was I thinking?

As the class concluded, I grabbed my dad by the arm and pointed to the prayer. A tear came silently to his eye as he read, *"LORD, let me feel the pain of others so I can pray as if it was mine."*

What have I done? *"LORD, let me feel the pain of others so I can pray as if it was mine."*

"LORD, let me feel the pain of others—" Enough! Enough. Must I feel every pain? Must I personally experience every loss before I can know it—before I can pray it? I can't. I can't bear any more.

Enough, God, enough. I can pray a lifetime on this pain.

WITHDRAWING PROTECTION

WHEN MY JIMMY WAS A LITTLE BOY, I STOPPED PRAYING for God's protection over him. I started to pray for his maturity. I stopped asking God to keep my boy safe and started asking to make him strong.

I had looked around me and seen parents segregating their children from society with expectations of keeping them from becoming "soiled" by the world. I saw children bound up like prisoners under their parents' protection, in hopes that this isolation would result in purity. I heard a new prayer mantra emerging: "Lord, build a hedge of protection around my child." The more I heard that prayer and the more I thought about that idea—that "hedge" mentality, that "hedge" theology—it seemed faulty to me.

As I reflected on my own life, I realized that my greatest growth had occurred during my worst droughts. My highest mountaintops were surrounded by my deepest valleys. Signs of maturity had always risen during seasons of trials and testing. It was common and consistent that my testimonies of increased faith were a result of God's *Presence through* my pain not His *protection from* my pain.

By asking for protection, I was depriving my son of pain.

By depriving him of pain, I was blocking him from God's Presence. I was sabotaging Jim's growth, his strength, and his maturity. So, I withdrew the protection.

As a direct result of his pain and suffering, my beloved son remains the strongest and most mature twenty-four-year-old I will ever know.

When my Jimmy was a little boy, I stopped praying for God's protection over him. I started to pray for his maturity. I stopped asking God to keep my boy safe and started asking to make him strong.

There are times, looking back from this vantage point, knowing what I know now, when I can't help but wonder if that prayer cost my brave boy his life.

IT WASN'T FAIR

WHEN JIM GOT SICK, HE HAD TO MOVE HOME. SOON ANNIE left her apartment and came home. Nate turned down a scholarship at a local art college so he could stay home. John was still in high school. All six of us were back under the same roof and surrounding Jim. As bad as everything had become, it was good to have everyone home.

Jim needed a separate room for his care and well-being.

Annie was a twenty-one-year-old who needed privacy. So John gave up his room to Jim and moved in with Nate in the basement. John lost his space. John, by all the rights and privileges of the youngest child and the last to leave home, should have had the whole place to himself. Now, he had no place to call his own. In the months that followed, we learned that cancer would give no rights or privileges to any of us. Nothing would ever seem fair again.

Shortly after Jim died, I had a deep sense that John needed his room back. He needed to reclaim Jim's space and make it his own again. I didn't feel ready to rearrange everything. None of us did. We still don't. I don't know when we will have the luxury of time and space to feel *ready* for anything again.

I've heard of parents who can't bear to see or touch their child's physical belongings for months and even years after they die. I've heard of parents who can't go into that child's room or even walk past their door. I've heard of parents who actually sell their homes and move because they can't cope with those physical reminders and sad memorials of their loss. I didn't have that luxury.

Only two weeks after Jim died, I boxed up his things and rearranged the room for John. All the reminders were gone. All the memorials were packed away. It was as if Jim had never been there.

IRRATIONAL ANGER

I'M ANGRY. I'M ANGRY ALL THE TIME. ALL. THE. TIME. There's a bitterness in me that could drive down a deep root.

I'm angry at everything, at everyone. I curse under my breath with no provocation. I make obscene gestures at no one in particular. I see someone laugh, I curse their joy. I see someone resting, I curse their repose. I see someone with a healthy child, I curse their wholeness. What gives any of them the right to laughter, health, or rest?

People tell me my loss is not all that bad, as if loss can be quantified or qualified. They claim others have it worse, as if there's some hierarchy of loss—some pecking order of pain. They say I should do this. I should do that. They tell me I should be better now. When were they appointed my counselors?

People go on and on about how good their lives are. They're relentless about how wonderful their children are. They brag about their daughter's accomplishments and boast about their son's potential. Where do they come off talking like that?

They're foolish—totally oblivious to the crushing sorrow that awaits them, completely blind to the unbearable grief that lurks in the inevitable shadows of their lives. They live with such apathy, such complacency, such presumption. How dare they?

Just wait, I console myself. They'll feel pain. Their joy won't last. Their health will fade. Their peace will wither. That'll wipe the silly smile off their faces. Break their arrogant pride. Who do they think they are?

Why do they deserve to be happy? Why do they have the right, and I don't? What happened to equality? To fairness? Why should *anyone* have the right to life if *everyone* can't have it? Why? Why doesn't someone say something? Why won't anyone give me an answer? Why?

Am I going crazy? Am I at the end of my rope? What would it feel like to fall? Have I already fallen?

GRIEVING? YEAH, GOOD LUCK WITH THAT

IT'S A CURSE TO BE BIG WHEN IT COMES TO GRIEVING. IT'S a disadvantage to be a man when you're sad. It's hard for a big man to find comfort. If you're a man, you're supposed to be tough. If you're big, you're supposed to be even tougher. If you're a man, no one understands you need to be held. If you're a big man, no one is able to get their arms around you far enough or tight enough to hold you—or at least enough to make you feel like you're being held.

After Jim died, I was expected to "be a man," to "get better" fast, and to throw myself into my work as if it was some sort of therapy—as if being busy would make me forget my pain. I was expected to "get over my grief" quickly and give one hundred percent to my work as if I had a hundred percent to give to anything. I was not allowed to grieve.

Then someone said, "Mike, as Christians we don't grieve."

So, I guess there's a third disadvantage to my grief—being a Christian.

WARNING:
If you are a
    large
        Christian
            man
                and you need to grieve . . .
well,
good luck with that.

AND THEN THERE'S US

WHEN DEATH RIPS A CHILD FROM A MOTHER'S ARMS, nothing can be made right with her world again. When death tears a son from his father's side, nothing can be made complete again. Perhaps there is such a thing as healing from pain or recovery from grief, but death is a wrong that can never be made right.

Death is our final enemy. We must not live under the illusion that we can "embrace" it and make it our friend. We can't be deceived into thinking that "misery loves company" and that the pain of death will draw us together. LuAnn and I cannot be fooled into believing that after Jim's death anything in our marriage will ever be as it was or will ever be as good as it could have been. Maybe something can be good again but, whatever "it" is, it will be good in an entirely different way than we can see now.

Jim's death didn't bring any new endearments to LuAnn's and my relationship. It didn't enlighten clearer understanding about each other's needs. It didn't add a higher level of care and sensitivity, dissolve our differences, or deliver mutual consolation.

Most marriages don't survive the death of a child. Many families crumble.

We must survive. I couldn't bear that loss too—the loss of marriage, the loss of us.

Never Give Up, Never Surrender

We live about four miles from Lake Michigan. The Great Lake is more like an ocean than a lake. *Unlike* the ocean, however, it has no tides, and its water is fresh. *Like* the ocean, its vastness is immeasurable to the eye and its waves can be gigantic. The Great Lake is rimmed with miles and miles of sandy beaches, rocky cliffs, and its famous dunes. Climbing a dune, whether its fifty feet or five hundred, is an exercise in futility. It's much like treading water. You don't completely sink but you don't get anywhere for all your effort either. To conquer a dune is utterly exhausting. Jim used to "run the dunes."

(Let me put that in a separate paragraph so you get the full impact.)

Jim used to *"run the dunes!"*

Jim's physical strength and stamina were phenomenal.

Any exercise you could imagine doing, he could imagine a more grueling way to do it. To watch Jim running the dunes would have looked comical if it wasn't so impressive.

The bowl is a huge, hollowed-out portion of a nearby sand dune. The prevailing winds off Lake Michigan have swept the sands upward to form the unusual phenomenon. Jim's *favorite* thing about the bowl was winter. With a blanket of snow covering the dunes, the bowl became the wildest ride in town. Jim and his friends would bundle up and declare, "We're going sledding at the bowl!" By sledding, they meant toboggans, saucers, sleds, pieces of cardboard—anything that would slide and slide fast. The only requirement was speed. Whatever got them to the bottom of the bowl the fastest was the best.

They would drop off the rim of the bowl at one edge and hope to get enough momentum to carry them most of the way up the opposite edge. Once momentum was lost and they came to a stop, they would pick up their sleds and trudge up the remaining distance to the opposite rim from which they had begun. Jim said the worst was to wipe out at the bottom of the bowl. That meant they had to climb *all* the way back to the top.

And wipe out, they did. Jim would boast that, "When you go sledding at the bowl, it's not a question of *if* you get hurt but *how badly* you get hurt."

That was Jim. He loved the thrills and spills of life.

Who could have ever guessed he would take the terrible fall into cancer?

August of 2004, while "running the dunes," the area above Jim's right knee began to bother him. He thought he had injured it. At that point, no one, absolutely no one, would have or could have suspected it to be the progression of a deadly tumor. As a fitness trainer, Jim attempted to tend the "injury" himself. Despite his best efforts, he was unable to combat the increasing discomfort and swelling. He never made an issue of it. He never complained.

He saw a couple of doctors and sports therapists during those months. He had x-rays taken. One weekend, unknown to his mom and me, it was bothering him so much he visited a local hospital emergency room. No one could accurately define his condition. No one could have imagined a diagnosis of cancer.

Jim had a Ewing sarcoma, an extremely rare form of cancer that most doctors will never see in their lifetime. We cannot fault anyone for a misdiagnosis. X-rays do not reveal sarcomas. An MRI can even appear deceiving to an eye that is not specifically trained. Ultimately, it's even possible for the multiple "stains" taken during the biopsy to miss a precise diagnosis.

It's impossible to know if Jim ever suspected anything of such magnitude. He was not a man given to worry, and he would never do or say anything to be a burden or a concern to those around him. Right up to the night before that dreadful MRI exposed his tumor, Jim was confident and consoling. "Don't worry, Dad," he said. "It's nothing. It's only an injury. I just worked it too hard. I should have rested it more. I should have been more faithful with the instructions the doctors gave me. It's going to be okay." Those words still haunt me and break my heart.

With that MRI, our worst fears were realized. Jim had cancer. We didn't know the exact strain, but we knew it was a sarcoma. We knew it was rare and extremely dangerous. The doctor who read the MRI told Jim that his condition was "grave." I watched as my son's countenance fell. His eyes reddened and tears began to well up. That was the first and last time I would ever see those emotions. I believe that, in that unbearable moment, Jim "set his face like flint" against his cancer. He never cried again. He never complained. He fought with a fury and determination that didn't know the word *retreat*.

The last couple of months, the largest tumors pressed hard against his spine. Nothing could relieve that pain. With anguish in his heart, he confessed, "Dad, I've never felt such pain." The last week of his life, when tumors had overtaken his lungs and the pneumonia had set in, there was a new sadness in his eyes as he asked, "Dad, how could I have gotten pneumonia?" That was it. That was all. There were no complaints. There was no fussing.

Jim never feared his treatments and never doubted his recovery. "Bring it on," he'd say. "Bring it on!" In the early days of his treatments, there was talk of amputating his right leg. Even then Jim responded, "Bring it on. Take my leg. If it takes the cancer, take the leg." Jim's cancer was his enemy, and he was going to defeat his enemy no matter what it took—regardless of the cost.

He never gave up. He never surrendered. He fought with all his might right up to his final breath. It never got the best of him. Jim kept his strength and courage all the way to the end. Then he laid down his life with unparalleled grace and dignity.

I still stand amazed at you, Jim. Utterly amazed.

OTHER PEOPLE, NOT US

TODAY IS THE FOURTH OF JULY. INDEPENDENCE DAY. Across the nation, through parades and fireworks, we, the American people, will celebrate freedom—a freedom that most of us didn't earn but all of us enjoy. Is it possible to fully enjoy or appreciate unearned freedom? Do those who fought—who struggled, who bled, who lost—do they appreciate it more and therefore enjoy it more? Though I don't know firsthand, I think they might.

I have wondered if those who suffered the high cost of freedom don't feel some resentment or even contempt for those of us who didn't—especially when they see how we take our freedom for granted and even abuse it. I think they might. I think I would if I were them.

Today is the Fourth of July. Thirty-five years ago, I was about to turn eighteen. It was during the Vietnam War. I remember the day I registered. I remember sitting in the local café with my buddies, hearing that our upper classmen's "numbers" were coming up. (Back then the lottery meant something wholly different than it does now. Now it means winning. Then it meant losing—maybe losing everything.) We listened for names and numbers. Listened as news came of selection, of deployment, and of battles. We listened as word of woundedness arrived. On one fateful night, we heard the unthinkable. One of our own, a hometown boy, had been killed. Then came a hero's welcome and a community funeral to honor the fallen. It didn't seem possible that something like that could happen to a young man from a small farming community so far removed from the rest of the world. And through it all, the numbness, the disbelief. This kind of thing happens to other people's friends, not ours. Right?

Today is the Fourth of July. Twenty-five years ago today, LuAnn's brother, Jim, was killed in a plane crash. He was twenty-four years old.

LuAnn and I were living in California at the time. We were watching *Ben Hur* on an old black and white television when the call came. In shock, we made arrangements to fly home. Later that day, as we were preparing for our trip, we went to the local grocery store. LuAnn fainted in aisle three. (She was five months pregnant with our first child.)

The paramedics came. And through it all, the numbness, the disbelief. This kind of thing happens to other people's brothers, not ours. Right?

During the remainder of LuAnn's pregnancy, we felt compelled to name our soon-to-be-born child James—in honor of her brother, Jim. Our feelings were mixed. At times it felt like it would be a fitting memorial. Other times it felt like it would be a frightening memory. As we approached the delivery, we had abandoned the idea and chosen a different boy's name. We just couldn't go with "Jim."

Delivery day finally came. Boy or girl, Jim or not, that baby wasn't going to cooperate. Rolled backward, upside-down, and weighing over eight pounds, there was no way this kid was taking the normal route—the prescribed path for entering this world. Finally, at 8:02 a.m., the cesarean incision was made, and a perfect little boy emerged. Immediately, the doctors and nurses started singing Happy Birthday. I'd never heard of such a thing and have never heard of it since. Between each line of the song, they called out, "What's his name, what's his name?"

> Happy birthday to you,
> *What's his name, what's his name?*
> Happy birthday to you,
> *What's his name, what's his name?*

LuAnn and I looked at each other. Our eyes met and we shouted in unison, "JIM!"

Happy birthday, dear Jim.

Happy birthday to you.

His name was Jim.

Today is the Fourth of July. Twenty-four years ago today, LuAnn and I celebrated our first Fourth of July with our nine-month baby boy, Jim. The doctors tell us now, that the abnormal cell that would ultimately turn to cancer and claim our precious son's life had already formed in his little body. His life had a time bomb ticking away.

Jim loved life. He celebrated life. If there was a party going on, Jim was in the middle of it. If there wasn't, he'd make one. He breathed life in with all his senses. He embraced life. He took in all the sights and sounds and smells. He drank every drop. He tasted life, and to him, it was all good. He loved rollercoasters, fast cars, loud music, and fireworks. He never missed the fireworks.

Today is the Fourth of July. Two years ago today, Jim was at the fireworks display. Last year he was too sick. Today he's gone, a fallen soldier, a casualty of war, a victim of cancer. Today I don't want to see any fireworks. I don't want to ever see fireworks again. Today, with sorrow heaped upon sorrow, I don't want to celebrate. I don't want to be happy.

I find myself resenting and even holding contempt for those who celebrate today—today and any day. They flaunt their happiness in front of me—happiness they take for granted, happiness they haven't earned, happiness they don't deserve.

And, through it all, the numbness, the disbelief. This kind of thing happens to other people's sons, not ours. Right?

An Appetite for Grace

I'M WEARY OF THIS WORLD WITH ITS WICKED AND SINFUL ways. My heart longs to be free of this world—to lose these chains and fly away. The things of this world hold less and less fascination for me. I am less attracted to its values and more appalled by its lusts. I despise my sinfulness. I deeply regret my sins. There is a new remorse that absorbs my soul, a remorse born of my present pain, a remorse that seeps out of my deep sorrow.

My pride has been broken. I would openly name my sins if I thought it would be beneficial. I refrain from that confession for fear of offending others, not for fear of humiliating myself. My arrogance has been shamed and my humanity shattered. I am devastated and deep in despair. I am tired and hungry.

I am acquiring an appetite for grace.

TAKING UP THE FIGHT

I HAVE EMPLOYED MANY WAR METAPHORS AND ANALOGIES regarding Jim. I speak of his battle, his fighting spirit, his courage, his never-surrender philosophy. His cancer was his enemy. He assaulted it with a warrior-like mentality. There was a morbid kind of propriety, even justice, that Jim died on Veteran's Day.

I want to take up Jim's fight. Not his particular battle against cancer but his ferocious fighting spirit. God put Jim at the battle's front, in harm's way, right in the line of fire. My boy didn't want to be there, but once in place he didn't flinch. He didn't retreat.

The place of honor on the battlefield of life is not necessarily a remote, unreachable tribe in Africa or a starving village in Bangladesh. The struggle is not only against injustice or violence. I believe the battle wages most within the soul. Life is first and foremost a spiritual battle.

I want to take up the fight. I want to make a difference. I want what I do with my life to matter. I want to help—someone, somewhere, somehow.

BEING IN THE BATTLE

SOMEWHERE IN JIM'S LAST DAYS, HE AND I WATCHED THE new classic, *The Gladiator*. As it concluded, he turned to me with a forlorn look in his eyes, and said, "I wish this was like that." By *this*, he meant his cancer. By *that*, he meant the sword. It made me angry—not the realism of the cruelty we had just witnessed or the reality of the human injustice. I was angry because *our* battle couldn't be fought like that. I would have given anything to have taken up one of those heavy swords and slashed away at Jim's enemy. I would have spent my last breath to conquer his foe. I would have beaten it down, and beaten it down, and beaten it down until all my strength was gone. I would have shielded him with my own body and ultimately taken the deathblow for him. I would have sacrificed everything—laid down my life to win the day—to save my son. I would have fallen on my own sword if I thought that would have changed the outcome. I would have, but I couldn't. I couldn't do that. I couldn't do any of that. *This* wasn't like *that*. That made me angry—angry at my own helplessness and my utter uselessness.

The ultimate battle is waged within the human soul. To confront and conquer the enemy there defeats death itself.

In the same way that Jesus's greatest battle was fought on the rough ground of Gethsemane, our greatest battle is fought on the treacherous terrain of the human soul.

"Father, Thy will, not mine." Jesus's words ring down through the millennia of time. I never heard Jim speak those exact words, but I also never heard him question why *he* was the one dropped on the frontline, why *he* was thrown into the midst of the "attack." He never questioned why that duty had been given to him and not the soldier next to him. He didn't retreat. He didn't call for reinforcements. He didn't ask to be relieved of his post. The irony of such valor and ultimate victory is that it is the result of personal surrender.

> *Dear God, I want to be like my boy. May I be as valiant. May You honor me, as You honored my son, and place me at the point of attack. May I honor You in my fortitude and faith as he did. And, when the end comes, bring me home to be with him.*

Needing To Hold Him

EARLY THIS AFTERNOON, FEELING LOST AND ALONE, I went to the funeral home where Jim's cremains are being kept. I asked if I could hold my son.

I was ushered to a quiet room and sat in a comfortable, over-stuffed chair. I was brought a heavy black container made of a hard, plastic compound about the size of a child's shoebox. An official certification on the side read, "The cremains of Jim Sollom." The attendant gently handed it to me and left me alone.

An unexplainable flood of an inexpressible something filled the room.

"Hi, Jim."

I cradled him in my arms.

I kissed him.

I cried.

I don't always know why I do the things I do.

A Place for Jim

JIM'S CREMAINS WILL BE BROUGHT BACK TO OUR ROOTS in Northern Minnesota and laid in the familiar soil of his ancestors. He will lie next to his grandmother in our family cemetery where the gravestones date back to the eighteen hundreds.

Our cemetery sits atop a sand ridge bordered on two sides with elms, birch, and evergreens. A white-railed fence runs parallel to the small country road that crosses over the ridge. The west edge of the cemetery opens to the vast fields I used to work as a boy. North of the cemetery is a gravel pit where I rode my motorcycle. Traversing the top of the ridge is one of those picture-perfect, two-track, grassy lanes that few know about and even fewer use. It became one of LuAnn's and my favorite places to sit and cuddle as high school sweethearts.

Our first-love kisses were shared on the very same hillside where our firstborn son will lie. It is a fitting place, but it is a spoiled treasure.

EXHAUSTION

IT WAS DISTURBING AFTER JIM DIED HOW EASILY PEOPLE dismissed the consequences of his long, exhausting illness. They were willing to accept how much his *actual death* drained LuAnn and me, but they had forgotten how fatigued we already were by the time he died. Terminal illness is absolutely draining.

Our loss, our pain, our grief, and our struggle began at Jim's diagnosis. It began the moment we heard the word *cancer*. No one seemed to comprehend that. I'm not sure we completely understood the cumulative devastation ourselves.

Too many people, particularly in the case of a long, drawn-out illness, speak too casually of death being the end of suffering. They speak too callously of death being the beginning of grief.

"It's so sad they died, but at least now the suffering is over."

"It's so tragic that they died, but at least now the grieving process can begin."

The death of my son was a paralyzing shift in reality—an agonizing tear in the fabric of eternity. The suffering wasn't over. It had just begun. The grief wasn't beginning. It was already ancient and heavy.

No Shortcuts

I READ BOOKS AND ARTICLES ABOUT GRIEF BEFORE I grieved. I have read books and articles about grief *since* I started grieving. Authors who write books about grief, *before* they grieve, draw insight from the valleys of others and have tried to convince me that it's not "all that bad." Authors who write books about grief, *after* they grieve, confess that it really *is* "all that bad." Drawing insight from the depths of their own valley, they try to convince me it doesn't have to be that bad for me. With the best intentions, they try to show me a shortcut.

Anything designed to shorten the path only serves to sabotage the journey.

This is my journey, and I must take every step. If I don't

get through all of it, I'll never get through any of it. There are no shortcuts.

People Say the Dumbest Things

"God never gives us more that we can handle," declared a would-be comforter.

I remember looking at him with a blank stare and simply saying, "What?"

Hoping to better clarify himself, he responded more loudly, "I said, God promises He will never give you more than you can handle."

I paused a long while before falling upon a numb reply. "I'm sorry," I said, "I don't even know what that means."

It was a cold, wintry night when we held "visitation" in honor of our blessed son. Before we left for the funeral home, I sat my family down and comforted them as best I could. I encouraged them to be patient and gracious as many people, friends and strangers alike, would be shaking their hands, embracing them, and trying to say something poignant and appropriate. I warned them that, though everyone's intentions will be to encourage, many will end up saying something clumsy and inept—something stupid and even hurtful. I encouraged them to be courteous and receive everyone's attempts kindly. I prepared them for:

God had a reason for this that you may never know.
You will either become bitter or get better.
What doesn't kill you makes you stronger.
Jim is in a better place now.
It's such a blessing that his suffering is over.
Take comfort; as Christians, you don't have to grieve.
It's not as bad as you think right now; time will heal.
Be thankful that you had him for twenty-four good years.
At least there are still three other children.
God answered our prayers; Jim has been healed.
You must be strong for the rest of your family.
God won't give you more than you can handle.

It's too easy to believe we can know something without having had firsthand experience. As a result, we proclaim our untested beliefs like a parrot, having no idea what we're saying. We end up blundering.

"God never gives you more than you can handle." What would a statement like that have meant to my son, to my mother, to my father, to my grandfather? All four died of cancer. In what way was their cancer *not* more than they could handle? Cancer took their lives. It killed them. How were they supposed to "handle" that?

Jim, in his wonderful optimism, would say, "I have cancer; cancer doesn't have me." Damnably, in the end, cancer *had* him. It got the upper hand, and he could no longer handle it—it "handled" him.

"God never gives you more than you can handle." No, there must be something better than that—something deeper, something stronger. There must be something better than foolish reasoning and feeble rationale. There must be something more than the false hope of "handling" death.

There was a significant amount of blundering throughout Jim's visitation and memorial service, but we all did quite well. The best words I received were from a beautiful little girl. Looking up at me with her innocent eyes, she pulled on my coattail and said, "You are sad your son died."

Tears filled my eyes. "Yes, I am," I replied as I knelt down to her. Wrapping her soft little arms around my neck, she proclaimed, "Me too."

Me too might be the smartest and most compassionate thing to say.

Still Holding On

JIM IS NOT COMING BACK.

A kind of insanity works its way into grief that holds on

to the belief that the one who is gone could come back. It's irrational. It isn't true. Jim isn't coming back.

I still haven't figured out how to live with that.

Last night, when I couldn't sleep, I sat in the den on "Jim's" recliner and fingered through scores of pictures—pictures of my boy when he was young, pictures of him when he was as old as he would get, pictures of him with family, pictures of him with friends, and pictures of him by himself doing the crazy stuff he did.

Last week, when I couldn't sleep, I opened the antique trunk where we have stored all Jim's keepsakes and baby clothes. I reverently removed and refolded everything.

Last month, when I couldn't sleep, I reopened the boxes in which I packed up Jim's room, more than eight months ago. I laid everything out and then repacked them.

Last winter, in the weeks after Jim died, when I couldn't sleep, I called Jim's cell phone over and over just to hear his voicemail message:

> *Hey, it's Jim. Leave a message. Later.*
> *Hey, it's Jim. Leave a message. Later.*
> *Hey, it's Jim.*

I listened to it over and over. That's gone now.

Last November, in the days after Jim died, when I couldn't sleep, I went to his bed and lay on his pillow. For many days, I could still smell him. I would lie there and breathe him in. Eventually that faded.

I miss my boy. I miss the happy sight of him,
I miss the special way he smelled, and I miss the
unmistakable sound of his voice.
I want my son back. I still want him back.
I will always want him back. Always!

People say I'm holding on too long. They tell me it's time to let Jim go.

They don't know what they're saying.

NOT WHAT I EXPECTED

Faith doesn't feel like confidence;
    It feels like fear.
Peace doesn't feel restful;
    It just feels numb.
Love doesn't feel like pleasure;
    It feels like pain.
Grace doesn't feel amazing;
    It just feels lonely.
Faith, Peace, Love, and Grace.
    They don't feel like I expected them to feel.
    They don't *feel like enough.*

No More Middle Ground

IT'S LABOR DAY. MY NEIGHBORS ARE FERTILIZING THEIR yards. That's the secret you know, fertilize on the holidays— Memorial Day, Fourth of July, and Labor Day. It's the way to a beautiful yard.

I don't care. At all. I don't care how my yard looks. Or how my house looks. I don't care how I look, or that I'm out of shape. I don't care that I haven't bought any new clothes for years.

I just don't care about any of that stuff.

Yet, I care so desperately about people—about my family, my friends.

I think what's happened is that there's no *in between* for me any more—no middle ground. Something either matters or it doesn't. If it matters, it matters so very much. If it doesn't matter, it doesn't matter at all—not even a little. I don't have the energy to care about the "in between" stuff anymore.

What Difference Did It Make?

WE DID EVERYTHING RIGHT.
> *We did everything the way "they" said we*
> *were supposed to do it.*
> *We did it all the best we could.*

Jim was conceived in love. LuAnn and I dedicated his life to God, through prayer, many times before his earthly life ever began. LuAnn had a healthy pregnancy. We went to Lamaze classes. We planned for natural childbirth. LuAnn left her career and stayed home to care for our newborn son. There was no television in our home. There was music and laughter. There was lots of love and affection. We prayed with our son and blessed him every night.

LuAnn breastfed our little Jimmy for as long as the "experts" recommend. He was raised during our health food days, so he grew up drinking raw kefir and juices extracted from an overpriced juicer. He ate fertilized eggs and fresh-picked, organically grown fruits and vegetables.

Jim didn't drink alcohol, smoke, or do drugs. He treated

his body like the temple it was. He ate well and lived well. He was hardly sick a day in his life. He was the picture of health.

Nevertheless, at the completion of twenty-four years and one day, Jim died of a rare "childhood" cancer. The doctors told us Jim's was an embryonic cancer and that he'd had it since before he was born.

> *We did everything right.*
> *We did everything the way "they" said we were supposed to do it.*
> *We did it all the best we could.*

What difference did any of it make?

THE UNCERTAINTY OF LIFE

THERE ARE MANY NIGHTS, DESPITE THE LEVEL OF MY exhaustion and the sedating promises of my medications, that I do not sleep. Last night was one of those nights.

I kept my vigil in the recliner where Jim sat and stared out the window where he stared. I wrestled with what he must have thought and how he must have felt. My heart broke as I imagined his loneliness, I wept as I imagined his fear, and my rage rekindled as I remembered his suffering. I struggled to identify with his battle and to once again take his pain to myself. I know it's futile, but I still long so deeply for him to live, for joy to return, and for life to resume.

As I peered into the dark last night, I thought about Jim's death. As the night wore on, I longed for rest and searched for memories.

Today is the eleventh day of September—9-11. Today is a day of solidarity—of a common loss, a camaraderie of shared grief. I feel that solidarity more today than any past "nine elevens." Sudden terror branded those infamous numbers into all our patriotic souls five years ago. I didn't know loss then. I know loss now. I didn't know grief then. I know grief now. I didn't know death then. I know death now.

9-11 ushered in a new reality of fear. We know now that no one is safe. No one is immune. No amount of past or present stability can be leveraged or bartered for future security. Life gives no guarantees—grants no special favors. We know now that unrest is no longer restricted to "distant lands."

9-11 changed us. It changed us all. Changed the way we look at today, the way we anticipate tomorrow, and the way we remember yesterday. It changed the way we will always remember two simple numbers—nine and eleven.

11-11 changed me. It's the day my son died.

9-11 and 11-11—they lie in wait for me, reminders of the instability and insecurity of this life. Reminders that no guarantees were given and no special favors were granted. Unrest has come to my "homeland."

LET ME COME HOME

Sweet Jesus, there is no rest here, is there?

You found none.

How did You put it?

The Son of Man has nowhere to lay His head.

I won't find any rest either, will I?

You weren't meant for this world.

Neither am I.

You have come into Your rest now, haven't You?

So, only in You will I find *my* rest.

I'm so weary, Lord.

Let me come home.

MEMORIES

I DIDN'T WANT SUMMER TO ARRIVE THIS YEAR BECAUSE it was always Jim's favorite season. Now, for the same reason, I haven't wanted it to end.

I didn't want fall to arrive this year either because it has always been *my* favorite season. It has always filled me with wonder—the cool air and vibrant colors. It's not my favorite season anymore.

Autumn now fills me with a new fear. Unwelcomed memories linger around every corner—memories of renewed faith in radical treatments that I know now would end in futility; memories of a final hope in an ultimate recovery that I know now would end in despair. This time of year now fills me with the dreadful reality that, in spite of all my prayers and pleadings, autumn would be Jim's last season—his last months, his last weeks, his last days, his last moments. Fall would be my last memories of my son's wonderful life.

SAD CELEBRATIONS

TODAY IS MY BIRTHDAY.

Happy birthday to me.

My heart has forgotten what it feels like to celebrate. Joy and happiness, fun and celebration, what were they? Where did they go? Pulled out from underneath me like an unexpected wave at early tide.

Our Lake Michigan friends don't understand tides—early or late. They sit at the water's edge from sunup to sundown without a care or concern. Their beach chairs are secure, their sandcastles are sound, their children are safe. No waves threaten them while they sit on shore.

Not so with the ocean.

Those who know will tell you, "Don't turn your back on the sea." It's true. I've witnessed the devastation when those words are not heeded. I've been the victim of those tiny yet effective tidal waves that sneak in and sweep everything out from underneath your feet. With sufficient ballast, I always remained unmoved and withstood the sudden waters, but I was still left cold, wet, and grasping to save all that was mine.

Despite anyone's best efforts to hold back the tide or stave the water's destruction, the waves came and what was left in their wake was only a shadow of what used to be—footprints washed completely away, carefully carved castles reduced to sea-soaked mounds of sand. Those wanton waves had no regard for the long hours the castles took to build or what a monument they were to a day well-spent with fathers and sons, mothers and daughters. The water simply did what water does. The waves did what waves do. The tide did what the tide does.

Perhaps you're reading this and have no idea what I'm saying. I've lived by the ocean and become acquainted with these waves. I've seen blankets, chairs, large coolers, and even small children picked up and swept off the shore in a matter of seconds by an early tide and an unexpected wave. It's sudden, it's terrifying, yet it's the regular rhythm of the sea. It happens every day.

I'm not talking about waves. I'm not even talking about water. I'm talking about my birthday. And the daily ebb and flow of life. You'd think we'd get used to them. They happen every day.

I sat with my family around the kitchen table this evening and celebrated the fact that I withstood another year. All the kids were there. Only *all* the kids *weren't* there. The absence of one was so present. We ate my favorite meal. I opened wonderful and thoughtful gifts from my wife and my children. We laughed. We cried. Another year gained. Another year gone. What an awful way to be reminded of my loss.

The sea snuck up on me again. Another tide has come and gone. Another wave has receded. That first sudden cold blast is over. My heartrate is slowing back down. I survey myself and my surroundings. Nothing around me is as it was. Nothing feels like it should. Nothing looks as it used to. A priceless treasure is missing—swept out to sea.

But I'm still here.

ANTICIPATING PAIN

SOMETHING HAPPENS IN THE HUMAN HEART TWO TO three months prior to a loved one's death anniversary. The days leading up to the day can be as bad as the day itself.

That day—and the anticipation of it—are like an hourglass. All the sand gets piled up, held back, squeezed off as it presses against the obstructed center. It's as if the opening is too small and all that sand will never make its way through the impasse. That's what anticipating this anniversary is like. (Anniversary—what an inappropriate title for such a terrible event.)

The sands of my sorrow have been accumulating. The hourglass picture gives some account for my growing anxiety. I've been getting worse every day. Tension has been increasing. The stress mounting. My fears have been escalating. My pain has been rising. My restlessness has been intensifying. I've been crying more and sleeping less.

The hourglass image has helped—a little. It hasn't made it any easier. It hasn't changed my feelings or lessened my fears. But it has helped me anticipate the feelings to come. I know it's coming—that awful, impossible day. Of course I know it's coming. How could I not? These days and weeks leading up to that unspeakable day hold incessant reminders of what lies in wait. We must all now relive what we never wanted to live in the first place. It's almost as if our beloved Jim must die again.

Time doesn't heal, doesn't forget. Time is the most unrelenting tormenter. A cruel barrier. It has severed me from my son's past, it separates me from his present, and it suspends me from his future. Time keeps us apart and refuses to reunite. We put too much hope in time—give it too much credit. Time does not heal. It does not forget.

Beneath that narrowing center, after the anniversary day, the glass widens to "open up" again. Things aren't better. They just "open up." Will that passage ever change? I guess only *time* will tell.

How Will I Know?

How do I know when it's time to stop? To stop this obsession—this incessant writing and journaling. How will I know when I've written enough? Written too much, gone too far? How will I be able to tell if the writing is no longer helping?

Am I dealing with my loss or dwelling on it? Am I healing my pain or enabling it? Am I closing my wounds or keeping them open? By concentrating on my sorrow, have I confined myself to it? Has my writing been therapy to protect me from my pain or has it made me a prisoner of it?

Has the time come for a change? How do I know? Can I just decide to rise up and feel different about anything? Do I have the ability to do that? Is it even my right to do that?

How will I know when enough is enough?

PAIN STILL CONNECTS

I'VE STARTED DREAMING. ACTUALLY, BETTER SAID, I stopped taking my medications so I dream again. I've always been a dreamer. The drugs numbed that. They dulled me and took away the dreaming. They helped me endure the days and sleep through some of the nights. They took the edge off. The problem was they took more than the edge. They cut into the core of me.

I felt better with the drugs, I admit that. I wasn't so anxious. I slept some. That was good. But I didn't dream. The drugs helped me bear each day and make it to each dawn, but I didn't feel like myself. I didn't feel like anything.

I didn't like that or want that. As a result of my drugs, I can understand addictions and the hold they have on their victims. I can understand liking and wanting the feelings those drugs bring. More than anything, I can understand being addicted to "not feeling."

But that's all I have left—my feelings, my memories, my sorrow, my grief, my pain. It hurts to remember. But remembering him is all I have left. My pain still connects me to my boy. Why would I want to dull that?

She Sat in His Chair

Jim loved to sit close to his mom.

LuAnn works from home as a medical transcriptionist for our local hospital. She sits at a computer ten hours a day, locked in her office, transcribing doctor reports. Jim wanted to sit next to her. The sicker he became, the closer he wanted to be to his mama.

We bought him a huge leather reclining chair and set it right next to LuAnn's desk. He loved it. It was oversized, soft, and comfortable. Jim sat in it all day and often slept in it all night. As the end drew near and his strength began to leave him, he never left his big chair or his mother's side.

After Jim died, LuAnn refused to sit in his chair. I wondered if I needed to dispose of it. It held such painful memories. Everything in this house holds painful memories. If I were to dispose of everything that holds a painful memory, we'd have nothing left.

There are floor-to-ceiling bookshelves in front of the chair and a small television tucked into one of the shelves. That little TV, several hundred volumes of classic literature, and Mom were Jim's constant companions.

In the evenings now, LuAnn and I sit in that room, watch

a little TV, and relax before we head up to bed. I sit in Jim's chair, and, though there is room for LuAnn beside me, she sits on the floor in front of me. It's been like that for a long time.

Last night she sat in Jim's chair with me. I didn't say anything. It was just good to have her by my side. I know she didn't do it easily. She didn't do it without grieving for her boy. But, she did it.

> She sat in his chair.
> > *That means something good is happening, right?*
> She sat in his chair.
> > *That means she's moving forward, right?*
> She sat in his chair.
> > *That means she's going to make it, right?*
> We sat together in our blessed son's chair.
> > *That means we're going to be okay, right?*

When we got to bed last night, we both broke down and wept. We both knew why. We still cry often, but it's been awhile since we've wept together. When the sobbing subsided, we were both overwhelmed with that familiar numb feeling. Some say that weeping has a cathartic affect. If that were true, we should be well-healed by now.

His Bright Eyes

JIM'S EYES WERE BEAUTIFUL—BRIGHT BLUE WITH A sparkle. They were striking, kind, and always strong and clear. Most people who remember him, remember his eyes—his eyes and his smile.

I received a five-page letter from a nurse who worked in the hospital where Jim spent the last week of his life. Jim's eyes, and the spirit that flowed through them, changed her life. The following words are from her letter.

> *You don't know me, but I work at the hospital. I was the one that found the extra recliner so Jim's friends could stay in his room. Before I start, let me just tell you that Jim affected EVERYONE that worked with him. He was amazing!*
>
> *I never actually met Jim or even talked to him. I came to work on Tuesday and found that there was a young guy on the fourth floor with terminal cancer. I felt sad, but honestly, didn't think much of it.*
>
> *During my shift I walked into Jim's room*

*to turn off the alarm on his PCA pump. Jim
was standing at the side of his bed, getting ready
to sit down. As I walked in the room our eyes
locked. I felt his split-second stare pierce my soul.*

That was it. That was all. A "split-second stare" from those
amazing eyes and her life was changed. In the remaining five
pages of her letter, that young nurse unfolded a wonderful
story of repentance, redemption, and a return to faith and
hope—not just for her but for an estranged friend that she
had reached out to with Jim's story.

She ended her letter with these words:

*I cannot begin to express the sorrow that my
heart feels for you. I cannot begin to imagine
how you, as parents, are feeling with the loss of
a son! I can tell you that this has affected many
lives. Jim had a MAJOR effect on everyone that
worked with him. Many, many tears have been
shed!*

As beautiful as her words were, they gave little comfort at
the time. They give some now.

ENTERING HIS SUFFERING

I'M SITTING IN THE BIG CHAIR WHERE JIM WOULD OFTEN SIT through the night. It's late. I have taken the sleeping aids my doctor prescribed for these times, but they will not work their wonders on me tonight.

As fate would have it, I am in the third day of a wicked flu. I say "fate" because of the poignancy of how it relates to my struggle on this night. It is, though weak in comparison, a cruel reminder of Jim's suffering. As such, I welcome it. With this misery, I enter into the pain and suffering of my precious son. I haven't felt the impact of that identification until these past three days. The vast difference is that I know my pain will pass. My son knew his would not. I know that my suffering is not unto death. My son knew that his was.

These past three days, I have experienced fevers, clammy sweats, and violent vomiting that left my core muscles and rib cage bruised and aching. I have been so nauseated and light-headed I feared I would pass out. I haven't eaten or slept. I have been weakened and exhausted by the ordeal.

This is what my son endured day after day, month after month. "Tumor fevers" raged in him, followed or preceded by cold sweats. Nausea hounded him constantly. He vomited so incessantly from his chemo treatments, it's a miracle he didn't wither away. He coughed so violently from the cancer in his lungs that he dislocated several ribs. The largest tumors pressed so hard against his spine that the pain could not be controlled.

This was my son's suffering, and for the last three days I have, in small measure, entered into it with him. I feel grateful somehow.

He Needed Me

I REMEMBER MY SON'S FINAL NIGHT IN OUR HOME. I remember the onset of pneumonia that night and his desperate struggle to breathe. I called his doctor for directions. He suggested we go straight to the hospital. My stubborn boy insisted he could wait until morning. That was one of my struggles—sorting out my role in the illness of an adult child. It was his life, his battle, his story, and, ultimately, his decision. From the first day to the last, Jim took responsibility for his life and his death. He never complained and never allowed himself to be a bother.

So, I sat with him.

No, that's not true. I sat in the next room. Jim never allowed his mom and me to "hover." So, I sat in the living room, answered him when he called, fulfilled his need, lingered just a bit, and then told him I'd be in the next room. As I sat, numb with fear, all I could do was stare at the clock and listen to his labored breathing. It was never more than ten minutes between his calls. I don't think Jim realized how relentless that night was. Each time, as the time before, I answered his call, fulfilled his need, lingered a bit, and returned to my perch.

In the early hours of the morning, he gave his final call. "Dad...dad!"

Quickly to his side. "Yes, Jim, I'm here. What do you need?"

"Company," was all he said. "Company."

In the late hours of the last night he would spend in his own home, my son gave his father the greatest gift. My brave, strong, independent boy needed me. He wanted my company.

In the midst of the suffering, my heart soared, if only for a moment. I sat with him, rubbed his back, stroked his arm, and silently pleaded for his comfort. He fell asleep. My baby boy fell soundly asleep under his daddy's touch just as he had done so many times so many years ago. I sat with him for the rest of the night. I no longer watched the clock. I watched my precious boy breathe.

I'm glad I remembered that. Maybe I will sleep tonight after all. My boy needed me, and I was there for him. As best as I know, I was always there for him.

ONE YEAR, ONE WHOLE YEAR

THE TIME HAS COME. THE DAY IS HERE. TODAY IS THE eleventh of November. My firstborn son, James Arlyn—my precious baby boy—died one year ago today.

I have lived for twelve months separated from someone I thought I could never live without. My life has endured an entire year devoid of one whose life was more important to me than my own.

I didn't want to live. So how did I endure? I didn't want to move forward. So how did I go on? And I didn't want this day to arrive. So how am I to bear it? Today, one year later, my heart still wants to believe Jim never left. Instead, I am forced to relive his leaving.

I know a father who lost his son. This father's son was a lot like mine. This father lost his son over a decade ago. This father said that after one year, the pain felt no different. It was less raw. That's all. Another father who lost his son told me that the second year was actually worse than the first. Other fathers who have lost their sons tell me that it was between three and five years before they felt like they could actually move on with their lives. All the fathers I know who have lost their sons say they'll never get over it. All the fathers I know who have lost their sons say they'll never get used to it.

I know a father who lost his son many years ago. On the anniversary date of his son's death, the whole family travels overseas. This father claims that none of them can bear to be in the same country much less the same town on that dreadful day. I can understand that feeling but I can't comprehend that luxury.

As I think about it, I wouldn't want to be gone. That would feel like leaving Jim to face this day alone. I didn't leave him alone a year ago as he faced this day, how could I leave him alone today?

In that bitter end, no matter how many friends gathered around him, no matter how close I held him, Jim had to walk into death's valley alone. I want to believe that in a "twinkling of an eye," heaven's hosts were there to meet and greet my son. But the loneliness still overwhelms me. I want to believe that on the "other side," God was waiting to welcome him. But from this side it still feels like God abandoned him— abandoned me. Will these feelings of loneliness and abandon ever resolve?

I wish I knew. I miss my boy so much it hurts. My arms ache to hold him. I still can't handle more than one day at a time. Don't ask me about the coming year. At least not today.

TWENTY-FIVE CANDLES

YESTERDAY WAS JIM'S BIRTHDAY. HE WOULD HAVE TURNED twenty-five. Today is the day he died. It's been one year.

Many weeks ago, as we began to anticipate this dreadful weekend, we set our hearts on celebrating Jim's birth and on commemorating his life rather than remembering his death. None of us want to remember his death. As a result, we gathered yesterday—his birthday—rather than today.

It was obvious who should be here with us. Jim had called five friends to his side when he realized his passing was near. We invited each of them and all of them accepted.

As I sit here in my favorite chair, the sound of our grandfather clock counting time in the background, a ray of sun shining through the window next to me, and the hour of Jim's passing approaching, I remember the events of yesterday's celebration with a quiet joy.

It was a beautiful day. I was raking leaves in short sleeves. The "kids" (our children and Jim's friends) started arriving around three o'clock. By five, they were all at the house. After lots of hugs and kisses, visits to what had been Jim's old room, and some general "roaming about," all ten of us headed for Jim's memorial marker.

The only marker, here in Michigan, is amongst many markers inlaid on a special memorial terrace near the entrance of the local college field house. It reads, "In memory of Jim Sollom, our beloved son." The forecast called for rain. We hoped it would hold off. It did not.

I lit a candle and set it next to our beloved's name. We ten comrades huddled close and held each other tight as the mounting wind and rain began to soak us. The tenacious flame, tossed about by the wind and pelted with rain, never gave up, never surrendered. We all thought of Jim's relentless fight.

We stood there for nearly a half an hour. Few words were spoken. Lots of sniffles. A "Happy birthday, Jim." An "I love you" or two. Mama's sobbing. My stumbling prayer. At last we walked away, each in turn touching Jim's name, kissing his marker, and saying good-bye—again.

As we gathered in our living room, the kids grabbed blankets and we all nestled in. I started a fire in the fireplace, lit several candles, and turned out the lights. Our meal earlier had been boisterous and filled with laughter, but everything turned quiet and calm as gentle memories filled our hearts.

A few choice stories were told with remembrances of good times and precious moments. As the quiet overtook the conversation, I continued to light more candles. The flames led us into a sacred silence. At one point, I took out my journal and read several of my more intimate memories. By midnight everyone was gone, leaving quietly with kisses and promises of undying love.

As I sit here now, treasuring the memories of last night, the moment of Jim's passing is nearly upon me. I just counted all the candles we burned last night. Twenty-five. I counted again. Twenty-five. Then I counted again. The same. I had unknowingly lit twenty-five candles.

Happy birthday, Jim! Happy twenty-five!

FAITHFUL ENDURANCE

THROUGH THE COURSE OF JIM'S ILLNESS, MANY GREW *impatient with being patient.* Many got *sick of someone being sick.* Watching people walk away—being deserted by his friends—may have been more difficult for Jim to bear than his disease. He commented that he was surprised by the ones who left, but he never named them. He didn't hold it against them.

An increasing number have also become *sick of someone being sad*—sick of *me* being sad, sick of *us* being sad. There are a faithful, proven few, who are still here and who we know now will never abandon us. The words *thank you* are far too poor to express our gratitude. For those who have departed, well, they aren't even reading this, so words would be wasted here. I confess, however, that I understand why they left us. I'm not sure I'd be any truer a friend if the tables were turned.

Were it not for my undying love for him, I could not have sustained his care. Had Jim not been my son, I could not have endured his illness either.

REMEMBERING

PEOPLE TELL ME THAT I NEED TO "FOCUS ON ALL THE good memories" of Jim's life, not the hard memories of his death. They don't know what they're suggesting. I can focus on the "good memories" of my mom's life. She was seventy-eight when she died. Though I wish I could have had her for another ten plus years, she had a good life filled with many good things. Recalling them endears her to me and commemorates the fullness of life. However, when I remember Jim and try to recall the "good times," I feel broken and overwhelmed with the emptiness of life. Every thought of the wonderful things he did just reminds me that he will never do them again—that he *should* be doing them still, but he never will. He can't. Not here. Not with us.

The "what was" can never make up for the "what will never be."

There *were* good times. I know there were. There *are* good memories to come, I'm sure there are. There *has* to be. I need time. I just need more time.

THE VALUE OF PAIN

DISEASE AND SUFFERING UNITE ME WITH HUMANITY. Healing separates me. Restoration would set me apart from all who continue to suffer.

Christian theologies contain suggestions of *divine deliverances* and Christian traditions are full of stories of *rapid rescues*. However, if these theologies and traditions of deliverance and rescue are misapplied, they become detrimental to the traumas and crises of this life because they not only promise healing, they promise the cessation of pain.

"Have faith and God will heal you from all the pain and grief and restore your joy," say my fellow believers.

The process of restoration does require faith, but it's faith to continue the journey, not faith to negate the necessity of a difficult step. Shortcuts misuse and cheapen both faith and forgiveness. They are forms of denial and escape. What is the final value of pain if it is only to be forgotten?

People would like me to circumvent my pain. Some desire so with a genuine care for me. They don't want me to hurt. Many desire it for themselves because they are uncomfortable with my pain. Sadly, the worst of the lot are my fellow Christians. They preach *quick healing* and *miraculous recoveries*—special interventions to nullify some of the steps that others must take. Why would I want to do that?

What would it prosper me, or anyone around me, if I skipped a step or two in my journey through grief and pain? If it is to speed up the process for the sake of someone else's comfort, then it is useless to me. I will inevitably have to return to that step at a later and more awkward time. If it is to relieve the pain for the sake of my own comfort, then it is selfish of me. I will never understand *my* journey nor be able to comfort *others* along theirs. If I let people rush me through this, I will inevitably end up pretending.

LOOKING FORWARD

"WHAT IS JIM SAYING TO YOU?"

This question came from a long-time friend.

What is Jim saying to me? Just to make sure I understood what she was looking for, I asked some qualifying questions. "Do you mean what words am I recalling from his life? Are you wondering if I'm uncovering hidden journals or the like? Do you think I'm having dreams or visions?"

Without commenting on those sources, she simply encouraged me to be alert to the many levels of consciousness in which Jim might be communicating with me or trying to communicate. I didn't know what to expect. I have longed for a dream or a vision so desperately that I may have overlooked other sources. Perhaps my friend was on to something.

I had some immediate impressions, but I told my friend I wanted to think about her question. I wanted to take time. I didn't want to respond with what could so easily be no more than what I *wish* Jim was saying. It would be easy to simply echo my own words and the words of others, not Jim's.

The remainder of that day was filled with making phone calls, scheduling meetings, writing, and running some errands. No thoughts came—even when I tried. Especially when I tried. It wasn't until I was driving home that evening that Jim broke into my consciousness. The words weren't audible. They weren't etched into the tailgate of the truck in front of me. However, they came to me that clearly and that profoundly.

> *"Get off your butt, Dad, and get moving."*
> *"Quit looking back. I'm not behind you, I'm ahead of you."*

That was it. But it was powerful. The words caused me to weep.

I don't know for sure what it means. It probably means a lot. Then again, maybe it doesn't mean any more than what it says.

> *My dear Jim,*
> *I'm going to do what you said. (As usual, you said it well.) I'm going to get moving. I'm*

going to quit looking back. I'm going to move forward. You've gone ahead of me. You've led the way. You've shown me the way. You weren't supposed to. I was supposed to go first. I was supposed to show you the way. This is so wrong. But this is what we have—it's all we'll ever have.

I'm tired, Son. I'm so tired. I'm tired of writing. You stir my heart. Words overflow. And I write. But I'd like to write of other things. I'd like to write from a different place. I'd like to write with my eyes looking forward not back— just like you said.

I love you, Jim. I love you so very much. I miss you so desperately. I ache to hold you. I long to see you.

Maybe you could ask Jesus to return more quickly. I would like that.

Love forever and ever,
Dad

MOVING ON A LITTLE

YOU MIGHT REMEMBER MY JOURNAL ENTRY FROM Easter Sunday and how I was unable or unwilling to remove the body of Christ from the cross on our family altar. I did so today. I removed the nails from His hands, wrapped His body in white linen, and placed it in the drawer.

I whispered to myself, "He is risen. He is risen, indeed."

I might be moving forward. A little.

New Fellowships

I'M A MEMBER OF A NEW FELLOWSHIP. IT'S THE FELLOWSHIP of people who drive Jeeps. Jim told me all about it. Now I'm trying to live it out. The membership is easy. Drive a Jeep. Drive a real Jeep. Not a soccer-mom, businessman, suburban-type, Cherokee version, but a real Jeep—a "Jeep, Jeep" as Jim used to say.

I drive Jim's Jeep now. I'm a part of that fellowship.

The dues for this fellowship are simple. Wave. Wave to other Jeep owners. It's not necessary to do anything fancy— no peace signs, hang-tens, or clenched fists. Just a simple wave will do. Raise your fingers off the steering wheel or drop your hand out the door. That's all.

I messed up a lot in the first days. Either I forgot, or I wasn't fast enough, or I just wasn't thinking. I received many waves to which I didn't respond. I'm better now.

Jim had a long list of stuff he wanted to do and things he wanted to add to his Jeep. Even when he was sick, he got a new front bumper and different fender flares. We worked together to attach them. Next on his list were a higher lift kit, a winch, a new back bumper, rocker guards, and a few performance boosters.

When Jim left us, he left me with his Jeep. In the beginning, I cried every time I sat in it and wept every time I drove it. But I was determined to make it mine—even though I will always call it Jim's Jeep. Every time I stepped into it, I was stepping into Jim's presence. I dreaded it. I longed for it.

For a while, I contemplated continuing Jim's plans and making the Jeep everything he would have wanted. I quickly decided I would rather leave it the way he left it. There's a dent in the front right fender from when he hit a deer. The front left fender carries a dent from when he lost control on the freeway and hit a snowbank. There's no rear bumper and the auxiliary lights, though mounted, were never hooked up. They still have two-inch lead wires hanging from them. Those wires will dangle there as a testimony to an unfinished life. Those lights will never shine. A lot of lights will never shine. The brightest light of all was Jim himself. The world is now a dimmer place.

I designed a personalized license plate for the Jeep. It says, LOVEJIM. It has two meanings for me. One is a declaration of my love for Jim. The other is Jim's final salutation to me; "Hey, Dad, here's my Jeep. Enjoy! Love, Jim."

I didn't want this fellowship. I inherited it through great tragedy. I receive it only to honor my son.

I'm a member of another fellowship I did not want and

find difficult to bear. The fellowship of fathers who have lost their sons—parents who have lost their children. The membership is unthinkable. The dues are unbearable. This fellowship numbers in the multitudes. We don't always see each other coming. There are no visible signs or identifiable characteristics. But, when I recognize them and they recognize me, we share a kind of wave. It's the tear in our eye that wells up so quickly. It's the "vocabulary of grief" that spills out so easily. It's a knowing embrace or an empathetic touch on the arm.

It's the Fellowship.

TOO BUFF TO GOLF

WHEN JIM GOT SICK, I WAS WORKING AT A SMALL manufacturing company. My fellow workers were extremely generous toward our family. Donations were taken for Jim, potluck lunches were held, vacation time was donated, and, in the culmination of giving, a golf outing was sponsored for Jim's benefit.

The outing was not only an affirmation of care, but the beginning of Jim's infatuation with golf. As a result of the benefit, Jim was completely outfitted with new clubs, a beautiful bag, and an assortment of accessories.

We all took up golfing, but few opportunities remained when Jim would have the strength to play a full round—even nine holes. We spent most of our time on the driving range. Jim's game was not finesse. It was all about power. All he really wanted to do was tear the cover off the ball. He was looking for the three-hundred-plus-yard drive. Every once in a while, he got it.

Even though chemo was ravaging his body and deteriorating his strength, Jim never lost his powerful physique. As he stepped up to the ball, with his broad shoulders and beefy arms, it was obvious that his body was designed for the beach, not the golf course.

He always was *too buff to golf.*

GO DREAMING

AS OUR FALLEN WARRIOR LAY DYING, HE DREAMED. EACH time he woke, we eagerly asked about where he'd been. Sometimes it was Disneyland. Other times it was the ocean. As those last torturous hours passed, he found it harder to pull himself out of his beautiful, distant dreams and put himself back into his terrible, present reality.

He would often talk bits of "crossover" from his dream until he came fully awake. One time he asked, "Where is that little Catholic girl who was singing?" It was no stretch for us to assume it was an angel.

It was heartbreaking on one such waking, after he realized he'd been talking nonsense, to hear him say, "Oh, I'm so foolish." I put my arms around him and assured him, "No, you're not, Jim. You've just been dreaming."

At another point, with halted speech as he struggled to breathe, our courageous hero whispered, "That's how…it's going to be. I'll…be dreaming. Then I'll…dream about heaven. And then…I'll see Jesus. That's how…it's going to be."

I pray that it was so.
I pray, that when the battle was over
and my brave boy had to go,
he went dreaming.

THE PERFECT WAVE

JIM'S CANCER CHANGED HIM. IT CHANGED ME. CHANGED us all. With amazing courage, Jim welcomed the change. He approved of the larger picture of his life. He stood firmly against his disease, but he rode the wave of change with fluid grace. His terrible trial deepened him, broadened him, and softened him.

One of the odd, yet obvious changes that struck me was

the walls of his bedroom. Throughout his life, Jim's walls were covered with a collage of sports heroes, fast cars, and rock bands. In the end, they were covered with intentional beauty, color, and purpose. There were landscapes of majestic mountains, seascapes from Australia, and tranquil hideaways in the Greek Isles. One wall had a poster of two climbers suspended precariously from a lofty precipice, attempting to reach a seemingly unattainable summit. There was a quote at the bottom that Jim loved: *Anyone who thinks the sky is the limit has limited imagination.* Carefully hung on another wall was his favorite poster of his favorite surfing movie that bore his favorite idea:

ENDLESS SUMMER:

In Search of the Perfect Wave

Jim rode every wave of his life with equal enthusiasm. He saw every wave as a perfect wave. Or, at least, he rode them as if they were. He even rode the wave of his cancer with intentions and precision. He never backed off. He never pulled out. He rode it perfectly—all the way to the *far shore.*

> *Dear Jim,*
>
> *Oh, how I love you! You were the sun itself. You brought such light to our lives. You always sought the best and brightest in yourself, and in others, and in everything you did.*
>
> *You truly were "In Search of the Perfect Wave." I'm guessing that by now you've caught*

that wave. Perhaps God used it to bring you to the shores of heaven.

Surf, my son. Surf the wave. Run, my son. Run and play.

I'll be home soon,

Dad

THE WEIGHT OF EMPTINESS

PEOPLE SAY I'M "DOING BETTER." THEY SAY I'M "BRIGHTER."

At times I think my life has changed some. I can find myself caught up in work or activities and realize I haven't been missing my Jim—not every moment. I can give myself to family and friends and recognize that my life could still have meaning—even without Jim.

I see my friends and smile, so they say I'm "brighter." I meet my family and we embrace, so they assume I'm "doing better." But then, out of nowhere, emptiness and pain collide with me—an emptiness that weighs me down and crushes me and a pain so deep and dreadful that it deadens all my senses.

How can emptiness be so heavy? How can pain be so numb?

I'm living in two dimensions.

I can be in the midst of a group of people, talking and laughing and celebrating their lives, when a switch goes off inside me. The sounds of their voices dull and fade into the background. Images become foggy. Distant and separate, I feel like I'm on the outside looking in. I turn invisible, and my mind shuts down.

I can be in the middle of a conversation with friends or family—engaging and enthusiastic. I can be all "bright" and "better." But the moment I turn to go, that switch flips off again. I become exhausted and deadened. Everything collapses as if I finally relinquished an awkward position I could no longer sustain. As if I released my grip on a heavy load I could no longer carry. Everything shuts down. Everything goes silent.

There is no "living with this," yet I live with it. There is no "bearing this," yet I bear it. I eat and sleep. I go to the store. I mow the lawn. But I do these things as nothing more than sustaining a habit.

I'm not "brighter." I'm not "doing better." I'm just learning to cover my pain and protect my burden.

Some days I whisper a curse in the madness of those moments—a curse upon myself for my obvious pretending and a curse upon everyone else for their apparent complacency.

The longer Jim is gone, the more I miss him. That doesn't go away. Not a day goes by that I do not miss my son. I don't get used to his absence. Time does not lessen my loss. Our continuing separation doesn't decrease my longing. I miss him every day—every single day.

What's wrong with everybody? Doesn't anyone understand this? Can no one hear my cry?

Listen to me. Hear this:

THE LONGER MY PRECIOUS SON IS GONE FROM MY LIFE THE MORE I MISS HIM!

FAIR WARNING

I WOULDN'T BELIEVE IT WHEN I FIRST HEARD IT. WHY would I?

Even with the testimony of those who have known it firsthand, I still couldn't imagine it. How could I?

I was warned, but I didn't know what to watch for. I was told to prepare myself, but I didn't know how. They said it was coming and nothing could hold it back.

Now it's here. Now *I'm* here. Now I know it firsthand. Now I can tell you it's true. But I still can't believe it.

The second year is worse than the first.

> *God Almighty, what's the matter with You?*
> *Do You really think this is all for my good*
> *somehow?*

*Is this supposed to make me love You more—
make me want to go on serving You?*

*Do You really expect me to keep pleading for
You to quench my thirst when all You ever do is
deny me a drink?*

I'm dying of thirst in this dry, forsaken land.

*The second year is worse than the first. It
makes no sense.*

No Songs to Soothe the Soul

I HAVE NO DESIRE TO RETURN TO REGULAR CHURCH
attendance any time soon. I say "regular attendance" because
I have made a few feeble attempts. I took John to our old
church a number of times after Jim died, and I have visited a
few new churches. It's just not the same. Something's wrong.

I'm sure it's *me* that's not the same. I'm sure that the
"something wrong" is with me. Nevertheless, I don't go. I just
don't belong. I don't fit. There's no place for my pain. There's
no room for my lament and languor. There are no words to
express my sorrow. No songs to soothe my soul. There is no
fellowship with my suffering. And little or no patience with
my grief or acceptance of my anger.

So, I don't go.

Last weekend, John graduated from high school. It should have been a time of great celebration. We were happy for our son—*our baby*. We went through all the motions. We all gathered for his big day. We were all there, but we weren't *all* there. We never will be.

> *Dear God, will we ever get past this? Will the best times always be the worst? Will the fun times always be the hardest? Will it always hurt so much to laugh?*

LuAnn and I attended John's baccalaureate service the night before his graduation. It was held in the same sanctuary as Jim's memorial service. It was the first time we had been back since that awful night. That was difficult. During the baccalaureate proceedings, a small group of graduates led a couple of "worship" choruses. One song kept repeating the line, "You give and take away. You give and take away. You give and take away...blessed be your name." I wanted to scream. I wanted them to stop. I wanted to slap them in the face for their ignorance—or maybe it was their innocence. "You give and take away." Did anyone there know what they were singing? What, if anything, had any of those singers had taken away? It was all so hypocritical. It was all so wrong.

Music—*church* music. That's one of the big reasons I don't go.

I Have a Proposal

Let's do this:

Let's make a new rule for church and for "church" people. No one can sing or say anything just because it's popular— even if it's true. They can only sing or say what they have personally experienced and even then, they can only sing it or say it if they can do so in a spirit of gentleness.

Let's outlaw clichés and forbid the recitation of conventional platitudes or the repetition of traditional inanities. Let's require that God's own words cannot be quoted outside of God's own story—the whole story. While we're at it, let's insist that life isn't a game and worship is more than entertainment. Let's say and do all that but then let's not hold our breath. It probably won't make any difference. Jesus Himself tried to set down some new rules but nothing seems to have changed.

I still say, "I lost my son" and "God took him." I'm so fed up with the pious, self-appointed counselors who feel they *must* correct me on my "poor" choice of words. I'll explode the next time someone says, "Oh, Mike, you didn't lose him. You know where he is." Or, "God didn't *take* him. He *received* him."

I'll blow up at the next person who "comforts" me with the stories of Job and Joseph. They were two guys like me, lost, destitute, and crying out for hope and salvation. Yes, I know that. But I also know the happy endings of their stories.

Of what value are these men in the midst of my suffering? Their stories may be unparalleled in their tragedy, but they are also unparalleled in their glory. These tales have happy endings, gold at the end of the rainbow, and clouds with silver linings. What comfort is it in my distress to simply tell me that everything worked out for a couple of *other* guys? I have read the Bible—the whole Bible. Everything doesn't always come up roses for everybody, every time. "Every silver lining has a cloud," seems to be a more consistent theme with many biblical characters.

Just once I'd like to hear my counselors speak to me of God's Presence with John the Baptist as he sat imprisoned on the eve of Herod's birthday—the day before he was beheaded—when he couldn't help but wonder if Jesus really was who he had always hoped He would be. Speak to me of comfort, hope, salvation, deliverance, and healing in that story. Then I'll listen.

LOOK AGAIN

WE ALL LOVE A GOOD JOB STORY, THE CLASSIC COMEBACK story of the guy who loses everything and faces every adversity but still endures. As Christians, we love the part where Job says, "Though He slay me, I will trust Him." We have no idea what that really means, but it's such a great line. We love the way Job's faith survives even when pushed to the edge of despair and the brink of death. Yep, it's a good story with a good ending. It ends happily as every good story should, and we love happy endings. We think they give us hope.

I don't like the story of Job. Especially the ending. As I see it, it is not a happy ending—not even close.

Look again.

It was one thing to take Job's possessions, his land, his livestock, and even his health. It was quite another thing to take his children. How is it we miss that? Everyone always misses that. In our exuberance over all the stuff of life, we can often miss life itself.

How is it that those who boldly proclaim the glorious ending of redemption and restoration and God's full restitution of all Job's wealth and power always miss the part about his children still being dead. He gets everything back, and more, but his children are still dead. In what kind of life is that good? In what kind of story is that a happy ending? In what twisted economy is that a fair trade? In what untested perspective of faith could that ever be seen as grace and goodness?

LIVING IN REMEMBRANCE

I DETERMINED SOMETHING TODAY. IF ANYTHING GOOD comes of this dark valley, I will not readily share it.

I will never share what comes of my valley with someone who is still in their own.

I will only share what comes of my valley with someone after they have come out of theirs.

I will only share the goodness that came from my valley if they have already shared a goodness that came from *their* valley.

I will only share *my* goodness if *their* goodness was greater than mine—more enlightening, more encouraging.

I will strive to remember what it was like to be where they are and, for their sake, I will be nowhere different—nowhere better.

If you don't understand what I've just said or why I said it, then I can only assume you have yet to walk through a dark enough valley. Part of me would like to just forget what I've learned and hope that no one ever needs to understand. However, another part of me has come to realize that people can walk through these dark valleys and still not understand what I've just said. Or maybe what happens is, after emerging from the dark experiences of life, they forget what the valley was like. They forget the pain. Or, perhaps, for the sake of survival, they mask the pain. They try to live apart from their pain. Even worse, they forget what it was like and start to parrot back those asinine comments that so infuriated them when they were in the midst of their pain—in the midst of their dark valley. They forget what it was like and start saying the very things they swore they'd never say.

I promise I will never do that.

As miserable as this feels, I don't think I ever want to live apart from my pain. I don't ever want to forget it.

If I emerge from this valley, I promise never to set myself apart from it or place myself above it as if my position represents some goal to be attained. I promise to always return to the darkest part of the valley in order to walk amongst those who struggle there. I will not stand aloof on the mountaintop, casting down a distant lifeline. I will plunge into the valley and "press upon" those weary travelers from behind and beneath.

I don't want to forget this valley—not in two years and not in twenty. Not ever. I don't want to forget the death of my son. I don't want *anyone* to forget the death of my son. If we did, it would be as if he never lived.

God doesn't want us to forget the death of *His* son, and I don't want you to forget the death of mine. If we forget the suffering and death of the Son of God, we forget the great gift of life. If I forget the suffering and death of *my* son, I will do the same.

So, lest I forget, I will live in remembrance.

I don't mind feeling sad, so don't feel sad for me or feel you have to make me happy.

ENCROACHING FEAR

I have lost my nerve.
I have lost my confidence.
I have lost my courage.
I am lost.
My heart is broken.
My spirit is broken.
My will is broken.
I am so badly broken.
I feel worthless.
I feel useless.
I feel insignificant.
I am irrelevant.

I appear foolish.

I appear lazy.

    I appear crazy.

I am confused.

I panic over anything.

I avoid everyone.

    I worry about everything.

I am afraid.

I am discovering phobias I didn't know I had.

I might be creating them.

    I guess I don't really know.

I am desperate.

No Longer Me

I WAS DESPERATE. MY SON HAD DIED, MY MOTHER WAS dying, my family was devastated, and I had just lost my job. The first thing I did was the last thing I wanted to do. I got right back on my feet and pressed on. I had no choice. I had fallen on hard times. It seemed I had fallen from grace. I had to be brave. I had to be bold.

Despite the grief and pain, I was "out there" every day— pounding the pavement, knocking down doors, and looking for work. I talked to anyone who would listen. I contacted everyone I could think of. I didn't leave one stone unturned.

Word got out. People wanted to meet with me. I was confident that I would get back on my feet again, that I would save my family from ruin, that I would renew my "calling," and that God—the God whom I had served for so long—would be faithful.

That was a year and a half ago. That was then. Nothing came of all that. I couldn't sustain it. I couldn't endure. I couldn't carry on. People were curious about my life, even enamored with my "story," but no one was truly interested in employing me. I fear that I was no more than an amusement to most.

Now I'm completely broken. Now I'm thoroughly lost.

How can I be more broken now, when I've worked so hard at mending? How can I be more lost now, when I've spent so much time searching? Don't I know how to mend or search? Am I trying to find something that can't be found? Am I trying to fix something that can't be fixed? Am I searching for the wrong treasure? Am I trying to mend the wrong break?

What's happened? What's the matter with me? Where did I go wrong? Why hasn't anything worked out? What am I trying to do and why am I so afraid to keep trying?

Who am I supposed to be now that I am no longer me?

An Unbearable Day

It's here again. Father's Day.

Years ago—another lifetime ago—when I spent most of my working hours on the platform, I hosted many Father's Day festivities. I sang songs, made commemorative speeches, and recited proclamations of love and honor. I believed I was a sensitive host because I always gave recognition and made accommodation for those to whom Father's Day wasn't a happy day. I always received gratitude from those people.

I knew that some sons and daughters had just lost their fathers and this was their first Father's Day without their dads. Some had grown up with stepfathers or surrogate fathers. Some with no father at all, and this day represented a lifetime of questions and loneliness. Some had cruel and abusive fathers, and this day only stirred up feelings of resentment and even hatred. I knew that some children's only image of a father was that of a complete failure or an utter disappointment.

I realize now that I always took the perspective of the child. I took that perspective because I had grown up as a son whose father had died. I never stopped to think what it was like to be the *father* in those Father's Day situations. I didn't know then what it would be like to be the father who had failed—failed to provide for his children, failed to protect his children, failed to raise them up in the way they should go, failed to nurture them into responsible adults, failed to keep them alive.

Today I know what that's like. I lost one of my dear children—my firstborn son.

I know what it's like to be the son of a dead father. Since I can remember I've danced around that black hole for fear of being sucked into the nothingness. The remainder of my life, I will know what it's like to be the father of a dead son. The death of my father defined the beginning of my life. The loss of my son will now define the end of it. My entire existence will be a dance around the same dark abyss.

This is my life. When I was a child, I lost my father. When I became a father, I lost my child. What intolerable bookends.

What an unbearable day this has become.

NOT WANTING TO FORGET

I SPENT THIS EVENING LOOKING AT PICTURES OF JIM. I have scanned several of them into my computer. I pull out that file almost every day and look at those images. I make copies of them, cropping them, enhancing them, and enlarging them. Sometimes I just zoom in on his face and get as close as I can. I can never get close enough.

It makes me weep.

One day, LuAnn came upon me when I was working on a picture of Jim taken at his favorite place—the beach. "What are you doing?" she asked. I instantly choked up, turned the computer screen so she could see, and said, "Holding our son." She cried. We cried.

After Jim died, I framed many of his pictures and spread them around the house. It was difficult, but I wanted to see my boy. One day, LuAnn confessed that seeing Jim was just too hard for her. I took the pictures down and put them under our bed.

I know it's hard to remember, but I don't want to forget.

So, I spent this evening looking at pictures of Jim. I spent the evening holding my son.

I still don't really know what I'm doing or what might come of what I do.

THE SMELL OF HIS SKIN

I HAD A DREAM ABOUT JIM. I HAVE LONGED FOR A DREAM, a vision, something to assure me that he is all right—to know his suffering is over, that he no longer "groans" with the rest of creation. I have longed to see him—happy, healthy, alive.

I had a dream about Jim. It wasn't really so much about him. It was more like a dream with Jim in it. He didn't perform any heroic acts, wasn't bathed in a glowing light, and didn't sit with me and share words of comfort. He didn't put his arm around me and assure me everything was all right. He didn't tell me how much he loves me, or whether he misses me, or forgives me. In fact, he didn't talk at all. But then, he never did talk much. I guess that hasn't changed.

Jim was one of many in the dream. I didn't know where we were, and I didn't recognize anyone else. Jim and a bunch of boys were playing a game. It was an active game. They were running all about. I didn't know if it was football, soccer, or some made-up game. I didn't see a ball or notice any boundaries. Jim was wearing a familiar pair of tattered old khaki pants. He was barefooted and, as always, shirtless. I was watching the boys play but I never took my eyes off my son. I didn't get a good look at his face, but I knew it was him. I knew him by the way he moved. I knew his gait—the way he walked and ran. I knew the shape of his body and the texture of his skin.

I knew that he knew I was there, but he didn't acknowledge me. It was as if he couldn't—shouldn't.

At long last, the playing stopped and the boys took a rest. Jim stood alone, surveying the field and admiring his other companions. I moved toward him. He knew I was approaching, but he didn't turn. I walked up directly behind him.

His hair had grown out. He was broader than I remembered. He was taller. My face came squarely to the middle of his back. I reached out and clenched my hands on his strong, broad shoulders. I pressed my face into his back and laid my cheek against his skin. I could smell his skin. I could smell my boy's skin. I could feel his strong shoulder muscles rippling under the grasp of my hands. I could feel the warmth of his body.

I could smell his skin.

Dear God, how I had missed him.

It was then I realized no one else in my dream knew Jim had died. I knew. He knew. But no one else. In any other dimension of reality, that would have made no sense but there, in my dream, it made complete sense—it was obvious, it was clear. It would be too difficult for the others to learn of his death. They just wanted to play. It was equally obvious why Jim couldn't acknowledge me the way I would have liked. That would have given away our secret.

Jim had come back just for a moment, just to play, and just to let his daddy watch him. He couldn't acknowledge me or speak to me. I knew I wasn't allowed to speak to him or fully embrace him. I was unable to see his face. It was almost as if he was in another state of being that couldn't be fully approached. I could see him, touch him, even smell him, but I could not have him. Nothing in my dream fully explained the need for the distance. However, I knew space was required and I respected it.

So, I simply walked up behind him, clenched his shoulders, pressed my face against his back, and smelled his skin. Then I wept. Jim knew I was weeping. I knew he knew I was weeping. In that moment my soul touched his and I knew he loved me. My love for him surged through me. Then the dream was over.

The entire experience lasted a fraction of the time it has taken me to write it. I have longed for another and another and another. For now, I must be content with this one.

Jim is alive. He's warm. He's fit. He's playing. His hair has grown back.

His shoulders are broader, and he's bigger than before. But he smells exactly the same.

Different Praying

I'VE PRAYED MY WHOLE LIFE, BUT I MUST HAVE BEEN doing it wrong this time. This time, when it mattered most, I couldn't get it right.

What was I missing? Was it a matter of asking differently? An issue of seeking different things? Was it a problem of wanting with the wrong motive? Did it have nothing to do with asking or seeking or wanting? Or had it nothing to do with me?

I asked. I sought. I wanted. I've never wanted anything more in my life. I've never sought more diligently. I've never prayed more fervently.

In my personal experience, prayer has nothing to do with asking or seeking. It has nothing to do with wanting. Perhaps it has nothing to do with me. It certainly has nothing to do with what I desire. It has nothing to do with my hopes, my dreams—my will.

What I got was vastly different from what I prayed for. What I asked for, I did not get. What I sought, I did not find. What I wanted, I was denied. I prayed and pleaded and begged and bartered, but my beloved son died anyway.

He died anyway.

So what did prayer have to do with anything?

My Chair and Me

I SIT LONG AND OFTEN IN THIS CHAIR—THIS BIG OLD recliner. It's my home within my home. A cabin in the forgotten wilderness of my memories. An oasis in the dry desert of my days. It is a tableland on the steep mountain precipice of my hopes and fears. It is a solace amidst the fierce landscapes of my soul.

This is *my* chair—*dad's* chair. No one else sits in *my chair.* Even first-time guests to our home instinctively know this is a "reserved" chair. "That must be *your* chair," they say as I invite them to sit and they veer off to something that appears more generic.

Maybe it's obvious since it's the biggest chair in the house and I'm the biggest member of the household. It's a recliner, and dads always sit in recliners. It's getting old and worn and *real* men don't mind things that are old and worn. Or maybe *I'm* getting old and worn and everyone just assumes the two of us go together—my chair and me.

The chair sits in the southeast corner of the living room. It's a quiet room. No one but me spends much time here. It's a good room—a cozy room—a comfortable room. It's nicely accented with lots of warm tones, rich wood grains, cloth pillows, and a finely woven rug.

My feet are up. There is a pillow tucked next to me. An old brass floor lamp stands just to my right between me and a sixteen-pane window. Ideally, the light should come from the left. I'm right-handed. One of these days, I'll switch it over, even if it doesn't look right.

On the center of the east wall to my right is a brick fireplace with a terracotta tile hearth. The mantel holds plants, candles, and a mantel clock with a note on the back, claiming to have been given as a wedding gift in 1911. A watercolor print by a favorite artist hangs above the mantel. It's a winter farm scene complete with falling snow. The only electronic device in this room is a small CD player whose speakers straddle the fireplace. It's rarely used. I prefer quiet.

Just off my left shoulder—under the front window, facing our typical, Midwest, tree-lined street—is our family altar. The rest of the room is furnished with chairs, tables, lamps, and a large Shaker coffee table. There's no television. Directly across from the fireplace, hovering over an antique-looking sofa, is another watercolor by the same artist. This one is an original. It's also a winter farm scene. I love winter scenes—especially in the summer. Another clock sits next to the painting. This one belonged to LuAnn's grandfather. The silver face has been painted over with a coarse brush and white paint. Black rub-on sans serif numbers replace the raised Roman numerals that were its original design. LuAnn's dad did all that in an attempt to "repair" the clock. It stands as a monument to the utilitarianism under which we were raised. We have escaped the staunchest of those practicalities and even nurtured a wild artistic gene.

My favorite wall is the wall that I face. It's the north wall. Its window looks over our backyard. It's possible that this is my favorite wall simply because it's the one I am most familiar with. The one I always stare at. I believe it's also my favorite because of what the wall contains. It holds wonderful memories and sad memorials. It is a wall of emotion. And remembrance. I love that wall, yet I fear it. It takes me places without my permission.

Against that wall, in the northeast corner of the room, is a walnut-grained baby grand piano. We all played. The kids all played, but they're busy now with other things. LuAnn used to play, but she hasn't the time or energy anymore. I played once, just as I played the guitar—once. I sang—once. I sang *and* played—once. I was nearly famous with my singing and playing—once.

My song is lost. If it doesn't return soon it will be forever gone. I will die with it still in me. My song will not be passed on.

Against the left side of my favorite wall is an austere yet beautiful grandfather clock that LuAnn and I bought for each other on our thirtieth wedding anniversary—the pendulum relentlessly and ruthlessly passes the time.

Hanging to the left of the clock is a twelve-string guitar—silent, unplayed, untouched—reminiscent of another life, another identity.

To the right of the clock hang two of my original pen and ink renderings—the remnants of an abandoned pastime. The most recent date on my drawings is 1981, the year Jim was born.

On the floor beneath the renderings, reaching up to touch their frames, is a Peace Lily—one of many given to extend sympathy and peace when our son passed away.

This is my fierce landscape. My desert. My wilderness. My valley. This is my home.

This is my chair.

PRECIOUS YET PETRIFYING

I DON'T WRITE MUCH ABOUT ANNIE'S DRUG ADDICTION. I don't know why. Maybe I fear if I write about it, it will be real. And I don't want it to be real. Maybe, in comparison to the death of one child, the drug addiction of another doesn't seem so bad. Maybe my heart is just so badly broken that it can't take on one more thing—it won't allow another sorrow to enter in.

Annie stopped by last night while we were sleeping. She changed clothes, used my cell phone, raided the refrigerator, borrowed a jacket from the closet, and sat in my chair.

When I woke up this morning, I discovered my cell phone unplugged. Downstairs I found a blanket on my chair. I looked in Annie's room and spotted the dirty clothes she left on the floor.

My precious girl was three feet away from me and I didn't even know it. She wrapped herself in a blanket and sat in my chair. Maybe she even slept a little. There is something precious about that—precious yet petrifying.

What was she thinking? Why didn't she wake me? Why didn't she ask for help? Where has she gone now? Does she have shelter? Where will my girl sleep tonight? My heart is breaking with unbearable thoughts. I fear for her safety and her life.

Does God fear for her life? Is He concerned about her safety? Does He care she's cold and alone? Does it matter to Him if she lives or dies? Jesus's own disciples asked Him, during a raging storm, whether or not He cared if they lived or died. Am I asking anything different? If Jesus's closest and most intimate companions weren't certain of His care and keeping, how can I be? Look where following Christ has brought me.

Dear God, this is a frightful place.

NOBODY GETS IT

THE LONGER THIS GOES ON, THE WORSE IT GETS. THE more time it takes to work through this, the more "friends" fall from fellowship and support. Nobody "gets it." Nobody gets "this"—this pain, this emptiness, this numbness, this loneliness, this futility, this I-just-don't-care-about-anything feeling. Perhaps no one ever will. Perhaps no one ever can.

There is no one who can fully understand my life in any more depth or intimacy than I can fully understand theirs. I know how it feels to be me. No one else does. I know what it feels like to lose my son. No one else does—certainly not the father who has not lost his son and sometimes not even the one who has.

I now know several fathers who have lost their sons. I have come to realize that I have little to no idea what that's like for them. I only know what it's like for me to lose my son.

Every loss is different.

Every father is different.

Every son is different.

Every father and son relationship is different.

Every family is different.

Every son's mother—every father's wife—is different.

Everyone loves differently.

Everyone cherishes differently.

Everyone treasures memories differently.

Everyone lives differently.

Everyone dies differently.

Nobody knows the differences.

Nobody gets it.

Nobody can.

Nobody will.

This is too intimate.

His Own Sacred Space

DURING A RECENT STAY BACK IN THE HOMELAND OF Minnesota, I encountered many friends and family—people who love me. They all wanted to know how I was doing. They wanted to know how I was coping with my grief over the loss of my son. It had been awhile since I had had to answer that question. Most people here in Michigan have moved apart from my pain and no longer ask. Most people have needed to get some distance from me in order to survive their own emotions. Those who still care see me consistently enough that it's no longer a common question.

As I attempted to form an answer to the question, I

found myself raising my arms slightly over my head and to my right, making the shape of a sphere with my hands, and replying, "I think I have found a special place—a Sacred Space—to hold him." I stated that the loss is no longer directly in front of my face, completely blinding my sight. As I said those words, I held my hand in front of my face to block my view. I explained that for many months the pain was so powerful and the absence so present that I couldn't see clear of it or beyond it.

In those first excruciating months all I could think about, all I could talk about, was Jim—his disease, his suffering, and his death. As I look back on those months it was, for me, like the phenomenon of an open-heart surgery survivor. They "have to" talk about their surgery. They "must" show their scar. I have experienced that curious reality many times throughout the years. In the early days of my loss, I was doing the same thing. I had to talk about Jim. People had to see my "scar."

It's different now. I don't talk so much about Jim. I don't recite his life. I don't comment about his cancer. I don't recount his death. Yet, at the same time, there is little if anything of importance in my conversations that is not influenced by and subjected to the strength of his life, the courage of his death, and the depth of my sorrow.

I no longer have that desperate, almost obsessive need to talk about Jim's battle and my loss. But I am forever changed by it, I am deeply inspired by it, I am constantly informed by it, and I am now consciously talking *out of it*, listening *out of it*, and living *out of it*.

Don't think for a moment that this means my pain is gone or even that my pain is hidden in this "holy sanctuary" of which I speak. For one thing, I go to that Sacred Space every day and, in a sense, call the pain forth. You also must realize that this place, if it is fortified with any retention at all, is done so only with my emotions and my will. There are still times when my days are lonely, my nights are dark, my strength fades, and my resolve falters to the point that my present moments can still crush me with a pain just as hard and heavy as the day it first fell upon me.

There are a select few with whom I disclose my pain, but their number is decreasing. I have placed Jim in that Sacred Space, and there are only a handful of souls who I trust to tread on that holy ground. I don't let everyone in. I no longer tell everyone my story.

For a long time, I told my story, Jim's story, to too many people. As a result, I have been rejected by many and ridiculed by some. Many people, completely competent in any other situation, have stumbled under the weight of my exposed vulnerability. Perhaps they still speak truth, but they no longer do so with generosity or empathy. They remain distant and even aloof from my pain. They stand in a place that is aloof and distant even from their own pain. Ultimately, it's their inability to expose their own pain that renders them ineffective counselors or comforters for mine. I can wish now that I had been more calculating with Jim's story and more careful with my heart.

Unfortunately, I wouldn't have known at the time to do this any differently. My life—all of our lives—are haunted with the "should haves" the "would haves" and the "could haves" that leave some false impression that we can actually go back to do life over again or we can now know with certainty that we have learned from our past and will not make the same mistakes again. We can't. We can't and we won't. We do not have the luxury of evaluating our days until after we have lived them.

As I look back upon my life, there are a multitude of things I *could have* and probably *should have* and, from this vantage point, certainly *would have* done differently, but didn't. For better or worse, I am who I am because of them and, maybe by grace, in spite of them. I daresay the remainder of my life will be pretty much the same. If I live to tomorrow or even another twenty years, I will no doubt look back on today with all of its faults and follies and make the same "would-have-should-have-could-have" statements as I do now about yesterday and about twenty years ago. Perhaps all I can do is find another Sacred Space in which to place all that—that undone, unfinished business.

I have pondered these matters for hours. This has been another sleepless night of wrestling and writing. I'm exhausted. My soul lies open to the Sacred Space. I miss my dear son so very much. I long to see him. I live in isolation with that longing. My grief is like solitary confinement. My sorrow is like a grave. No one, not even my beloved wife, the mother of my son, can enter my tomb. It is a dark and lonely place. I feel the pain most at night.

It's now three o'clock in the morning. A great American novelist once declared, "In a real dark night of the soul, it's always three o'clock in the morning."

What a coincidence.

HOME FROM THE FRONT

GOING THROUGH THE RAVAGES OF INTENSE GRIEF CAN BE likened, in some ways, to coming home from the frontlines of a war. I confess I don't know what it's like to come back from combat, but I have heard the testimonies of those who have. Those who have survived battles bear witness to many of the same emotions and experiences that I have encountered on my journey with grief.

As soldiers have returned from the frontlines, they report many, or all, of the following realities:

✓ They are changed forever.
✓ They never get over what happened to them.
✓ The war never goes away.
✓ They cannot wipe out their memories.
✓ Normal life seems trivial.

- ✓ They don't have the same interests as before.
- ✓ They must tolerate the stupid and inept comments of those who pretend to understand.
- ✓ They have to put up with the complacency of those untouched by war.
- ✓ Bystanders seem clueless.
- ✓ No one understands what they've been through.
- ✓ They don't feel like they belong.
- ✓ No one feels their pain.
- ✓ Most people don't want to hear the raw truth of their experience.
- ✓ Everyone eventually expects them to be able to break free of the war.

My son fought a fierce and brave battle against cancer. His mother and I fought alongside him. He didn't make it. He didn't come home. He fell on Veteran's Day, November 11, 2005. As we endure that battle, we bear the realities and the emotional scars of what we saw, of what we had to do, and ultimately of what we lost.

The journey is long and hard. Be patient with us—you who have not been to the frontline, who have seen no action. We went somewhere we didn't want to go. We've seen things we never wanted to see. We've done things no parent should ever have to do. And then we had to leave our brave sweet boy behind.

Jim Has Come Home

I HAVE WANTED TO BRING JIM'S CREMAINS HOME FROM the funeral home. LuAnn has been hesitant so, for many months, I have denied my feelings and let him lie in a vault at the funeral home. I asked LuAnn what her reaction would be if I told her I had already brought them home. Reluctantly, she said that would be okay. I assured her I hadn't done that yet but that would probably be the way in which I would accomplish the task—I would simply do it without pomp and ceremony and without telling her.

I have done that now. I brought Jim home. He rests in a heavy black box in a miniature cedar chest I built in high school which sits under our family altar. That small chest used to hold old black and white photos of our ancestors. I guess it has always held our past. It has always held our humanity—our mortality.

A gravestone has been designed and will be set in place in our family graveyard on my childhood farm. Someday soon, we will bury Jim's remains. The difficult question, as we plan that day, is what should we do and how shall we do it? What kind of ceremony should we have? Should we even have a ceremony? Who should we invite? Who should talk? What should we say?

Should we sing?

The Best Times Are the Worst

It's Christmas Eve. Everyone's in bed. I can't sleep. I sit alone by the fire, remembering the events of the night. Our kids were here. We ate. We opened presents—good presents, thoughtful presents. It was a good night.

Last night, LuAnn and I wrapped presents for our children to put under the tree. We wrapped our children's presents and then we wept. We wept again tonight. We will weep again tomorrow. How can we not?

It will always be like this. Joy will never be complete again. Happiness will always bring pain. The fun times will always be the hardest. The best we can imagine will always remind us of the worst that has happened. Our worst nightmare has come to be.

Through the years, there have been difficult times and dark nights when LuAnn and I would comfort ourselves with these words: "At least we all have our health." During those times, when it appeared that our best dreams might not come true, we consoled ourselves with the fact that neither had our worst nightmare. That is no longer true. The very worst has happened. Our greatest fear has come to pass. One of our precious, beloved children is dead.

So, this is Christmas.

What a dark and lonely night.

No One Is Safe

ANNIE WAS REAR-ENDED TODAY BY A SPEEDING CAR ON the open road. She's shaken up, but she's okay. It could have been bad. She could have lost control. She could have been killed.

She's home now. She'll take a hot shower and something for the aches and pain. She'll get hugs from her mom and instruction on how to follow up with her insurance tomorrow from her dad. Hopefully she'll sleep. She's safe now, and for that I'm thankful.

But she's not safe. None of us are. My family is not safe. I'm not safe. My heart is racing. My head is pounding. I'm a wreck. There'll be no sleep for me now. This was the last thing any of us needed tonight.

I'd like to have a good day for a change. I'd like things

to go right for us just once. We're good people—my family and me.

Some families live charmed lives. I know those families. They aren't better than us. They aren't more devoted or wholesome. There's no reason why they should merit God's good favor. Some of those fortunate folks tell me there's no such thing as luck, that everything came to them by God's design. I tell them to thank their lucky stars that God's design hasn't required the life of their children. I tell them to be grateful for their good fortune in not having to encounter God's dark side.

So many bad things have happened to us. Why?

I don't think the world has come up with a good answer to that question. I doubt I'll come up with one tonight. Unfortunately, I suppose I'll try.

How To Be From Here

Here I am. It's a new year.

I don't want to start a new year. I don't want time to move forward. It's just moving toward destruction. Toward old age, poor health, pain, fear, and more loss.

Time moves away from my precious Jim. It moves away from my memories of him. I don't want time to come between Jim and me. I don't want to forget him or become accustomed to not having him here.

I don't want it to be 2008. This year will mark three years since Jim died. I don't want to say it's been three years since my son died. I don't want other people to say it's been three years since Jim died, implying that I should be over it. But they *will* say that it's been three years and they *will* imply that I should be over it. And I will resent them because I'm not over it. I will never get "over it." Why would I want to get over it?

"Forget his death and remember his life," say the voices of inexperience. Arrogant statements from ignorant onlookers will be my lifelong bane. Of course I remember his life, but each remembrance of his life is a reminder that he no longer lives. He lives in heaven, yes, I want to trust in that, but he doesn't live with me. That's the difference. Those who have never lost may never learn. I should give up on hoping they ever will.

Unfortunately, it didn't matter that I didn't want the New Year to come. Time has never answered to me. The New Year has come. It's 2008. This year will mark three years since Jim died. It will mark two years since Mom died and fifty-three since Dad. It will mark eleven years since we relocated to this desolate place.

Have I survived all that? Survived all these years? Have I survived anything? Have I survived the deaths of my parents? The death of my son? Long-term unemployment? I don't know. What does it mean to *survive*? I'm sitting upright. I'm dressed. I'm drinking a cup of hot coffee without burning my tongue, and I'm coherent enough to write. I'm in my right mind. At least I think I am. So, something survived. But I don't think it was me. I don't think the man I used to be survived.

But here I am. It's a new year. Perhaps it's a new me.

LONGING

WHY DOES GRIEF FIND US IN THIS PLACE? THIS PLACE so quiet and peaceful, so removed from everything we try so hard to remove ourselves from. Why must our grief find us even here?

LuAnn and I are the only guests at a cozy bed and breakfast. It is our belated Christmas present to each other. Our room is comfortable and serene. It's why we come here—peace, quiet, separation. We can pretend to be anywhere in the world. We can pretend nothing matters and all is right with the world. We can pretend none of this ever came to us.

We come here regularly—twice a year at least. It is our one indulgence. We read. We sleep. We love. And we weep. Dear God, we weep. Even now, as I sit beside a gentle fireplace, a cup of fresh coffee at my side, my body warm from a hot bath, I hear the muffled cries of my sweet wife in the other room. She's turned the jets on in the hot tub to mask her sounds, to protect me from her sadness, to be alone in her sorrow. I can hear her still.

My love for her calls to me to both leave her to herself and to hold her close.

My heart breaks—aches for her pain. She suffers so. Must she suffer so?

What does she long for? What do I long for? How can our sorrow be stilled? How can our emptiness be filled?

We long for mercy.

We long for hope.

We long for peace.

TRY AS WE MIGHT

THE FIRST TIME WE WENT AWAY AS A FAMILY WITHOUT JIM was less than four months after he died. It was Easter. A sympathetic acquaintance gave us the use of his family's lake home. It was a wonderful log home located on the shores of a small lake. I'm confident the house was beautiful. I'm sure the location was stunning. We just couldn't see it. Our pain was too raw. Our hearts too broken. Our vision was too clouded.

An island sat in the middle of the lake. A paddle boat lay on the beach in front of the cabin. Early one morning, the kids paddled out to the island. As our three children floated away in a boat built for four, LuAnn and I wept. We wept.

The empty place was more than we could bear.

It was a beautiful cabin on an amazing site with a fantastic view but, try as we might, we couldn't see it. We didn't want to be there. We didn't want to be anywhere.

LAST BREATH

JIM'S LUNGS WERE SO FULL OF TUMORS AND FLUID THAT he could barely breathe. Every gasp for air required a convulsion of his whole body. Despite his great effort, each breath took in less and less air—less and less precious oxygen. That's why he needed the mask. That's why he needed the oxygen. That's why we couldn't get him home for his birthday. No one had a portable machine that could feed him enough pure oxygen. He needed so much and was getting so little.

The nurses had been coming and going from his room all day and night that last week. They had been taking his oxygen mask off every time they gave him medication. They had been coming and going and taking off his mask for lots of reasons.

But that last day was different. They weren't taking his mask off that last day. They were no longer giving him medication, taking his temperature, or checking his vital signs. In fact, the nurses weren't coming into his room at all. No one was coming in. "He was actively dying," they told me later. There was nothing more they could do. And so, they left us alone. Everyone left us alone.

Food had been brought and laid out in the adjoining room. With much coaxing, LuAnn and the kids and Jim's friends went next door to eat. It was the perfect time for me to clean Jim up, to wash his face and hold him close.

And there he died. Cradled in his daddy's arms, he drew his final breath.

His battle was over.

My brave, sweet boy was gone.

A KIND OF MADNESS

WISHING YOU WERE DEAD TAKES A TERRIBLE TOLL ON your life. By that I don't mean the offhanded comment when you've been utterly embarrassed or when your high school sweetheart breaks up with you just before prom. I mean the real-life longing to die.

Grief, heart-wrenching grief over a deep loss, plunges the mourner into an insanity that leaves very little to live for. It's a kind of madness accompanied by a sincere, if not desperate, desire to die—to be with the one who has died.

The depth and breadth of this insanity is totally incomprehensible to those who have never truly lost or never truly loved.

I have been to that place—that insanity, that madness—that place where I wanted to die.

You don't come back from that place the same.

NOTHING CHANGES

DEAR GOD, CAN'T YOU WITHHOLD ONE BAD THING— *just one?*

Shouldn't something be getting better—anything?

Will nothing in this life ever resemble what it was—nothing?

There is not one evil thing that I cannot imagine appearing at my door. I expect nothing but loss, nothing but more tragedy, nothing but one grief heaped upon another and another and another.

All is lost. I lie in my bed feeling more dead than alive. The futility of rising every morning drains me before the day has begun. By midday my energy is spent. By night, despair has engulfed me. Sleep eludes me. My demons haunt me. My anger devours me. There is no deliverance for me from this world.

I am utterly alone. My children are lost to me. My wife is far from me. My "calling" is severed from me. My friends are disappearing around me. My confidence has abandoned me. My hope is gone within me. Nothing remains of my life that holds value or even interest to me. I have nothing left to offer this world. This world has nothing to offer me.

Today is December 31. Tomorrow, whether I want it or not, another year will impose itself on this already tired and groaning creation. It will not represent new beginnings. It will not offer a fresh start. It will not bring a second wind. It will not return my son to me.

Nothing will change. Nothing ever does.

Sweet Jesus, must everything die—everything?

ARE YOU?

Are You there, God?
When the night is long, the room is dark, the house is empty and a cold wind blows through my hollowed heart...
Are You there?
Are You able, God?
When no one seems to give a care—not for me, not for true and even if they did it wouldn't really matter . . .
Are You able?

Are You with me, God?

> *When everyone around has deserted to safer ground*
>> *and the emptiness is so void of presence I can hardly breathe . . .*
>>> Are You with me?

Are You listening, God?

> *When the silence drowns out my screams and my whispers*
>> *and all my best-chosen words shatter like the Madman's Lantern . . .*
>>> Are You listening?

Are You watching, God?

> *When it doesn't seem to bother You whether I stand or fall*
>> *and falling would seem to me, at least, at last, a welcomed relief . . .*
>>> Are You watching?

Are You willing, God?

> *When I'm at the end of all things human and divine*
>> *and I've given up hope that even You would want to help . . .*
>>> Are You willing?

Oh God, I'm desperate.

> *I really,*
>> *really need to know...*
>>> Are You? Are You God?

FROM THE DEPTHS

GOD ALMIGHTY! GOD ALMIGHTY! I CRY OUT TO YOU FROM the depth of my confusion—from this darkness, this emptiness, this loneliness.

I know You, God of Absence
I know You, King of Silence
I know You, Taker of Life
I know You, Spoiler of My Treasure
I know You, Lord of Abandon
I know You, Withholder of Grace
I know You, Remover of Peace
I know You, Prince of Pain
I know You, Lord of Loneliness
I know You, Captain of Strife
I know You, I wish I did not.

I wish I had never come to know You...You *Other God*.

I preferred the tame, safe, predictable God.
I preferred the meek, mild, definable God.
I preferred the quiet, calm, containable God.
I preferred the God of my youth.

I preferred the God of my innocence.
I preferred the God of my ignorance.
Return me to *that* place, *that* person, *that* God.
Return me to the God who would never leave me.
Return me to the Hope that would never fail me.
Return me to the Love—

>> the intoxicating,

>>>> irresistible love

>>>>>> that would never hurt me.

God Almighty, God Almighty, God Almighty, why do I still cry out to You? Why do You still remain silent?

THE LOSS OF COLOR

AUTUMN HAS BECOME BLACK AND WHITE. THE SPLENDOR of the season is lost on me. The wonder of color fades into shades of grey. I have noted the change of season, but it's not like before. It's still my favorite time of year and I still love it, but not like I used to.

The rustling leaves sound cozy and familiar. The cool air smells fresh and clean. And the slowing pace brings a feeling of hush and melancholy. All those autumn sensations are still here—just different somehow.

The crispness has a dull edge. The sights and sounds are

muted. The autumn air that once breathed new life into my spirit now hangs heavy around me. The thickness makes me weary. My movement is cumbersome. My breathing is labored. Some days I can't move, I can't think, I can't breathe. Some days I get stuck, pulled down into the quicksand of grief. The heavy memories this season holds weigh me down.

Memories are cruel tyrants. They take away all my freedom because they don't let me choose which ones to dwell on or when. Not that I want to forget anything. I don't. I want to remember. It's just that some days I'd like the ability to choose what I remember.

Today is one of those difficult days.

It took almost two years for us to find the courage to lay our brave, sweet boy in the ground. Jim died November 11, 2005. We had him cremated on November 16. Nearly two years later, we committed his ashes to the cold Minnesota soil. It was a Saturday—October 20, 2007.

As I write this, it's October 20, 2009. Today is a difficult day with memories too hard for me to remember.

Yet, I remember.

BEING CRUCIFIED

SINCE I WAS A YOUNG MAN, I HAVE BEEN TOLD THAT Christians are to be crucified with Christ—that we are to "die" and that we are to "die daily." I learned to recite those sentiments of self-sacrifice.

I heard those words. I repeated them. I espoused to the notion of being crucified. But I never had a clue what it meant. If we who claim the name of Christ truly knew what it meant to be "crucified," we would realize that we've never done it and never want to.

My son died after a ferocious battle with cancer. A parent's worst nightmare of the suffering, and death of their child doesn't come close to the reality of it. Believe me.

After my son died, I endured many stories from parents whose children *almost* died. I assume it was their attempt to identify with my pain—or make me *think* they identified with it. One father actually said, "I know *exactly* how you feel," and then proceeded to tell me how his son *almost* died. I heard of near fatal accidents, life-threatening illness, and last-chance, life-saving surgeries. I listened to story after story of how other parents' children *almost* died. I wanted to scream.

I would gladly sacrifice my own life to have had my son *almost* die.

My son didn't *almost* die. He died. And I have died every day since. I have spent nearly a decade dying every day. Actually, that's not true. I have spent every day wishing I could die. First, wishing I could die to take my son's place and when that didn't work, wishing I could die to join him. Actually, that too is not entirely true. It's less like wanting to die and more like simply not wanting to live. It's a subtle difference, yet pretty much the same.

I have lost everything during these years. My arrogance and my self-serving have died. My sense of safety for myself and my family has died. Feelings of confidence and security have died. Safety is an illusion. Pride is a lie. It also died. It needed to die.

I came close to "dying every day." Or as close as I would ever want to come. I didn't like it. It was awful. It's not something to take lightly or speak of easily.

We romanticize the notion of "being crucified with Christ" and think it's an attribute or characteristic we can add to our spiritual resume. We believe it's a tactic we can employ to enhance our testimony. "Crucifixion" is not an attribute or a characteristic or a tactic. It's not. We think somehow that it is something we can do *for* ourselves and *to* ourselves. We cannot. Like Christ, we are crucified at the hands of others. In many ways we are crucified by life itself. Like Christ, ultimately, God crucifies us. And, like Christ, our role is surrender. Surrender, not self-sacrifice. Self-sacrifice is still something we do *by* ourselves, *to* ourselves, and, ultimately, *for* ourselves. There's way too much "self" in it. Self-sacrifice is a subversive act of self-serving. Surrender is different. (How it's different is different for everyone. But that's a different conversation.) Surrender yourself completely to God and to the service of others and this life *will* "crucify" you every day. You will have nothing left to call your own.

And you won't like it.

You won't want it.

You'll wonder why you ever thought you would.

Broken Blessings

Blessings abound on the holidays. Everyone is thankful for family, friends, and another year of God's good favor. Christmas cards and Christmas letters list all the great and wonderful events and accomplishments of the past year. If the sender is a person of faith, the good tidings are punctuated with phrases like "Praise the Lord," "Glory to God," and "We are so blessed."

This season of "Happy Holidays" has skewed everyone's notion of what it means to be "blessed." It excludes the blessing of the brokenhearted. If there is any allusion to being broken during the holidays, it is only spoken of in the past tense, after it has resolved into a blessing.

Words of lament and languor are never found in Christmas letters. Those who are suffering deep pain and loss don't send Christmas cards. They wouldn't know what to say.

In the early years, my family and I sent Christmas cards and letters—usually creative and entertaining. Then, for many years, we didn't. I didn't want to tell everyone what was *really* happening in our lives, and I didn't want to pretend.

I didn't know what to say. I certainly couldn't refer to our lament and languor with a word like *blessing*.

I have often wondered what an honest Christmas letter would have sounded like these past years . . .

> *Dear Family and Friends,*
> *Life goes on the way it has for the past seven years. Jim is dead, Annie is still an addict, and the boys seem lost and wandering.*
> *Most days, LuAnn and I would rather die than live with the brokenness of our grief and loss. But, at least it's just most days now and not every day like it used to be.*
> *Merry Christmas and God bless you all.*

I think you get the idea. The deeper the wounds, the more the wounded retreat to the safety of "the cave." They don't send Christmas greetings. If any message escapes the confines of the cave, it's not a coherent blessing. It's broken and cryptic.

Here's the reality of caves and of blessings—a reality that has come to me slowly and I still hesitate to share: As a long-time "cave dweller," I can tell you that the cave is not entirely without its blessings. There are always blessings, but the blessings of the wounded are deep and dark blessings. They are hidden blessings. Broken blessings. They aren't the joy-filled, Gospel-y blessings that everyone wants to hear. They are unspoken and unspeakable blessings.

There is a language of "the cave." It's a language of languor and lament that most don't understand—a language that is offensive to the ears of the unwounded and the unbroken. It's not the language of Christmas. Or is it?

Have we forgotten the pain, the filth, and the fear on that first Christmas? Have we forgotten the tyranny, the scandal, and the destruction that surrounded and followed that humble and holy event? Have we forgotten all the slaughtered babies and the wailing mothers and fathers?

I wonder what Joseph and Mary's early Christmas letters would have read like. Any blessing they would have shared would have come from a dark and dangerous place.

> *Dear Family and Friends,*
> *Shalom.*
>
> *We are so self-conscious as we travel during this time of the year. It's obvious that Jesus is the only boy His age. People look at Him and wonder how He survived the slaughter. They suppose He must be older than He looks. They assume He must have been three or four when Herod had all the two-year-olds and under slain.*
>
> *Sometimes we fear the probing eyes and possible accusations. What if we are found out? We want to feel grateful and blessed that Jesus is alive, but our blessing has come at such a high cost to so many.*

How could those new parents claim a blessing in the face of so much brokenness? Did they feel blessed? I'm sure they did. The Son of God had survived the attempt to destroy Him. Mary was blessed. Holy Scripture calls her the most blessed of all women. But that blessing came from a place of grief and brokenness. She would not have spoken that blessing in the face of those who had lost so much—in the faces of the mothers who had lost their sons.

Jesus knew the "blessing of the broken" and didn't hesitate to assure all who could hear that there will always be a deep blessing reserved especially, and perhaps exclusively, for those who are broken.

Those who are poor in spirit
Those who are mourning
Those who are gentle
Those who are hungry and thirsty
Those who are merciful
Those who are pure in heart
Those who are peacemakers
Those who are persecuted
Those who are insulted
Those who are falsely accused

If we insist that life must always be a movement from brokenness to blessedness, we suggest that there are no blessings for the broken. It becomes easy to assume that because my neighbor's children are all alive, that my neighbor is blessed and I am not. It's easy to believe that because my daughter spent many years as a drug addict while other daughters were getting their education, getting married, and beginning careers and families, that those fathers are blessed and I am not. It is, in fact, easy to suspect that I am cursed. I must be. How else can my life be explained? It's easy to accuse me of much wrongdoing and faulty living. How else could such terrible things have come to me? Anguish turns to anger as the inequity buries every hope of what might have been.

It's Christmas Eve as I write. No one's home. LuAnn's working. Ordinarily, she'd be in her home office, but she has her rotation at the hospital tonight. Annie and John are in Seattle with Nathan. I sit alone with my thoughts on this most silent of nights.

Joy to the world because the Lord has come, but I feel only a flicker of that Presence tonight. My children are together. They are laughing. I know they are laughing. That brings joy to my heart but tears to my eyes. It is a blessing, but it's all still so badly broken.

> *Dear Christ of Christmastide, will this night ever hold the joy it once held? Will peace ever return to my world? Will hope ever find a place in my heart? Will I ever be able to accept the reality that my life is not going to be the life I had planned? Will I ever be able to live in a new reality of what my life could still and yet be? Will I ever accept my brokenness? Settle in it?*
>
> *Will I ever send another Christmas letter?*

HONEST COMMUNICATION

I SAID F*** YOU TO GOD.

It was a Sunday morning. My son was dying of cancer. At the time, I didn't realize he was in his final days. He was very sick that Sunday. He couldn't be left alone. I had decided to go to church. LuAnn stayed home to watch our dear boy.

As Jim's condition worsened, it became increasingly difficult to go to church—not just because we came to feel our place was at home, caring for our son, but because there no longer seemed to be a place for us at church.

I ventured out. As I recall, it was a dark and drizzly morning. Or maybe it wasn't. All those days were dark and drizzly. As I drove, I became caught up in deep and desperate thoughts.

The "numbness" which would be our constant companion for many years had begun to set in. As I drove, I became lost in thought and almost dangerously oblivious to anything around me. Unaware of my delusion, I was falling into an abominable stupor—my subconscious building terrible scenarios of the "not yet." That happened to me often in those final days. I would find myself in the middle of morbid thoughts about Jim's death—how he would die, who would speak at his memorial, where we would bury him. Eventually, awareness would burst into the middle of my stupor, and I would stop my treason. I loathed that kind of thinking. Shame consumed me. It made me feel like I was giving up while Jim was still fighting so courageously. I would shake off my feelings of guilt and all but curse myself for my betrayal.

On this particular Sunday, my mind had wandered down a particularly despicable path. When "awareness" finally hit me, I was shocked and appalled at where my mind had taken me. This was where I found myself:

> Jim had died. I was addressing a group of people. I had published a book about Jim— about his battle with cancer and about my journey through loss. I was lecturing and ministering about grief. *I had parlayed Jim's illness and death into a career.*

I personally know people who have done just that. I've watched as "survivors" write a bestseller about their heartbreak and go on the road with a successful speaking tour. That disgusts me. I don't even like to hear speakers use their family members in sermon illustrations much less expose stories of family tragedies. And there I was, turning off Sixty-Fourth Street onto Blue Star Highway, daydreaming about doing that very same thing. I had done what my heart so bitterly despised.

In that moment of realization, as I ripped myself from

the clutches of those thoughts, I seethed with anger. I was furious with God. Absolutely furious!

"F*** you!" I said to God. "Don't you dare use my son in that way! If he dies, I'll curse you! If you take my son from me, I would rather spend an eternity in hell than give you one more ounce of my devotion!"

If prayer is an act of open, honest communication with God when all the religious rhetoric and poetic language falls away; if prayer is the absence of false façades where even the most protected secrets are laid bare; if prayer is that moment of instinctively turning to God even when God doesn't seem to be anywhere in sight—and I believe it is at least that—then I did something new and profound on that dark and drizzly Sunday morning. I said f*** you to God. It might have been the first time I truly prayed.

Looking for a Reason

THE PARENT WHO HAS LOST THEIR CHILD ISN'T LOOKING for a reason—not in the form of an explanation. They know, without knowing why, there is no explanation that will suffice to comfort their pain or condone their loss.

The parent who has lost their child isn't looking for a reason why their son or daughter would have had to die; they're looking for a reason why they should have to go on living.

Unkind Words from Untested Voices

It's best not to comment on the depth of the water or the strength of the current while standing safely on the shore. Only those who tread the torrents of this life can comprehend the dangers and counsel those caught in the undertow.

I learned the hard way that those who have never experienced deep loss believe they have the right to bring criticism and counsel as if they have. Professional clergy run a high risk of that error in judgment. Granted, some of the best counsel I received after my son's death came from pastors and Christian friends, but they were also the source of the worst—the most insensitive and the most cruel. The most hurtful words leveled upon me in my grief were from an ordained pastor—one trained to give care and show compassion.

Many clergy can be profoundly intelligent and deeply chaste but lack comprehension of the human condition or even simple common sense. That's not entirely true. It's not that they lack *comprehension*. They lack the *courage* to be vulnerable and real about that comprehension. I say that with humility because I am an ordained minister—a professional clergy. Before suffering years of my own personal loss, I was equally guilty of counseling and consoling with untried equations and empty clichés.

My arrogance was born of ignorance, but it was still unkind.

HORRIFIC HONOR

THERE MUST BE A UNIVERSAL TRUTH REGARDING THE JOY a parent receives when they have a direct involvement or impact in their child's life. There is an equal pride when a parent witnesses the results of that involvement in their child's actions, attitudes, and character. It's the best of parenthood.

I have thought that, as an artist, athlete, and musician, there could be no greater satisfaction than coaching my children in these endeavors. I have thought that, as a Christian, there could be no greater joy than leading my children to a saving faith in Jesus Christ. I have thought that, as an ordained minister, there could be no greater privilege than officiating at my children's baptisms and weddings.

I have come to know that as a father, there is no greater, though horrific, honor than watching my child die.

Sweet Jesus, did I actually say that? What kind of awful grace has been at work in my soul?

It was an honor to watch my son die. He did it with such grace and dignity; with such strength and courage.

We only die once. There is no practice run. There is no

rehearsal. No prior experience prepares us for that final act. Regardless of the character by which we live, our true character will be tested once and for all when we die and even *as* we die.

I was able to show Jim how to throw a football, paint a portrait, strum the guitar, love a woman, and pray for grace to live. I was unable to show him how to die. He did that on his own.

If I die with only a portion of the grace, dignity, courage, and strength I witnessed in my son, you will think me valiant.

NOT HANDLING IT

WHEN I REFLECT ON THESE PAST YEARS, THERE WERE times I almost didn't make it—when I almost didn't endure. I wanted to give up and give in. Many times. Most times. I wanted to run away, as far away as I could run. There were times when I wanted to do great harm to a number of people and when I thought I was capable of doing great harm to myself.

Now, several years later, people seem to think I'm managing quite well. Many people now confide in me about their own struggles and trials.

I was recently in such a conversation as a friend exposed

and expounded upon a number of deep concerns over serious health issues amongst his family. As he did, he made the comment that he was "very tenderhearted and didn't do well with those kinds of issues." He recollected my loss at that point and added, "I know that I could never handle the death of a child." A twinge of resentment coursed through me. Did he actually think I "handled" the death of my child? Did he think I'm not "tenderhearted" or that I "do well with those kinds of issues"?

We have another friend who, whenever a comment regarding Jim arises, will literally flap her hands, as if waving off the topic, saying, "I don't want to go there. I wouldn't be able to bear such a thing." Does she think we "wanted to go there"? Does she think that LuAnn and I were "able to bear such a thing"? Does she think we're bearing it now? People can be very self-centered and self-preserving when approaching others' pain.

Are we "handling" it, "bearing" it? Hardly. And it's made more difficult by these sorts of friends who refuse to "go there" with us.

I still "go there." There are still moments, years after Jim's death, when the weight of my grief and pain crushes so heavily upon me that I can hardly catch my breath. There are still times when I feel the sting of my loss so sharply that it seems like yesterday. There are still times when I feel my heart pounding so rapidly in my chest that I wonder if it will burst. I'm still not "handling it."

People who hear me talk or write—if anyone ever hears

me talk or write—will think I've gone mad when I say things like this. They will say I've lost it—lost my faith.

I've done everything *but* lose my faith. Maybe I've finally found it. If realizing we can no longer "handle" this life isn't faith, I don't know what is.

IMPOTENT MONSTER

SOMEONE RECENTLY ASKED ME HOW I COULD MAINTAIN my faith without a deep understanding that God is all powerful and in complete control of fulfilling His purpose in this world. They asked how I could maintain my faith without the deep conviction that my son's death was a part of God's plan and accomplished according to His perfect will for my life. I told this person it was not only impossible for me to understand those things about God, but that those concepts were totally irrelevant to me. They didn't like that.

Jim is gone. It doesn't matter if any one of three or more different theories or theologies can explain it. No explanation will bring him back or cause me to believe my other children are safe. No mere clarification of God's ways will maintain my faith. It seems irrelevant whether God is in complete control or completely out of control because, despite all our fervent prayers and tireless efforts, Jim died anyway. God's involvement also seems irrelevant because neither God's complete control nor absence of control will guarantee my other children will live.

If *complete control* is so arbitrary and unpredictable, how does that differ from *no control?*

Even the best explanations as to how God was involved in my son's suffering and death only result in God appearing impotent or monstrous. Only God knows what was in His heart and mind regarding these things. Words like "plan" and "purpose" fall pitifully short in providing even the slightest comprehension or comfort. Maybe they're the right concepts, but I think the words are wrong.

I expect that I will see all things clearly when, at the end of all things, I am reunited with Jim. But then, of course, explanations will be even less important and even more irrelevant than they are now.

FALLBACKS

I MENTIONED EARLIER IN MY JOURNALS HOW LUANN AND I would comfort ourselves during difficult times and dark nights with these words: "At least we all have our health."

We also consoled ourselves throughout the challenging years of raising four teenagers, when it seemed like everything was going wrong. "At least they have their health." We could always fall back on that. Then our blessed son fell victim to cancer. We lost that fallback.

I've lost all my fallbacks. I can no longer trust God for the health and life of my children or that of my beloved wife. As I grow older, I realize more and more that I will not be able to trust Him for my own health and life either. How can I be entirely sure I can trust Him for my redemption? How can I be entirely sure I can trust Him for anything? How many times can I get the rug pulled out from underneath me and still believe the floor will hold? It seems even more futile when it apparently doesn't matter that I have spent my life in faithful, full-time ministry. God was unwilling to barter my lifelong devotion for the longevity of my job, the security of my home, the safety of my family, or the life of my son.

So, can I claim hope, or is all lost? Hope is not what I hoped it would be. I think I might hate hope. With its terrible, pseudo-optimism, it taunts and teases me with what has ended up as nothing more than shattered dreams and broken promises.

I wanted hope to be more than that. I wanted to be able to see it and feel it. I wanted to find confidence and certainty in it.

I wanted that for faith and peace too—and love.

THE UNCERTAINTY OF OTHERS

ANOTHER CHRISTMAS IS BEHIND US. WE HAD A wonderful time with the kids. They are generous givers. It was fun to watch them open gifts from each other. It was a good Christmas as compared to the last few. However, I confess I am glad the season is over.

I am glad to be done with the "well-wishers." That sounds awful, doesn't it? It seemed, more than last year, that people weren't so much "wishing me well" as "wishing I *was* well"— even demanding that I *be* well. I sensed more pressure this year to be over my grief or at least, not to bring it up. Three people in particular were quite persistent in goading me into being *grateful* for all that I have been given, pressing me into confessing that everything that has happened to Jim and to my family was a part of God's perfect plan, prodding me to admit that God doesn't make mistakes, and pushing me to acknowledge that I am now able to see a greater purpose in our suffering.

It perplexes me as to why that is so important to people— why it's so important for them to believe those things and why it's so important for them that *I* believe those things. It seems to be of first importance to them. (If there's one thing that we Christians have in common, it's that we all disagree on what's most important.) It's as if the uncertainty of their faith has to be bolstered by the certainty of mine.

Why don't my "advisors" try to reassure me of God's love for me and my family even during these most difficult days? Convince me that God's grace will ultimately be sufficient to get us through this. Why don't they try to persuade me that even in the darkest night I am not alone, or encourage me that, even though God's creation has gone terribly wrong, He will win out in the end? Why is it of such a singular importance to convince me that God did all of this by design and that it all fits into His perfect plan and I must, therefore, be grateful for all the atrocities that God has done?

This has unsettled me.

LOOKING FOR SUPPORT

I WAS RECENTLY POINTED TOWARD A GRIEF RECOVERY group at a local church. I knew I had to do something to break loose of my grief, to get a job, to get better. I had to do something. I hesitantly, even reluctantly, attended a meeting.

I came in quietly and didn't say a word. I barely looked at anyone. I felt certain that if I opened my mouth or met another pair of grieving eyes I would explode. When the coffee break came, I made a run for the door and swore I'd never return.

Two weeks ago, I returned.

I wrote the following "story" expecting I would be asked to share it with the support group. I was never asked to share. That was okay with me. I don't expect that I will return again.

> My name is Mike. I'm a father who has lost his son.
>
> My wife, LuAnn, and I lost our firstborn son, Jim, after a fierce battle with cancer. He died in my arms on November 11, 2005, the day after his twenty-fourth birthday.
>
> Following Jim's death, much like wounded animals, LuAnn and I clawed and crawled through the first days and weeks. Our best hope was to "survive" the holidays, get to the beginning of a new year, and reach the quiet protection and safe cover of our "cave" to begin some kind of healing.
>
> What met us at the beginning of the New Year was the termination of my job. Declaring that the depth of my grief rendered me incapable of fulfilling my work requirements, my employer of eight years fired me.
>
> Shattered by the betrayal, I stuffed my grief, bit my bottom lip, and began an ag-

gressive job search. Four months later, on the first day of May—May Day—my mom died. Two weeks later I crumbled.

I have little to no memory of that summer, the summer of 2006. The pain numbed me. The emptiness crushed me.

My other three children and my wife have all suffered in their unique and varying ways. My wife is a long way from being able to attend these meetings or encounter a support group like this one. She still hopes to wake up to find this was all a terribly cruel dream.

My children seem lost and lacking focus since their big brother, their anchor, their champion, was taken from them. My other boys, Nathan and John, don't talk about Jim very often but when they do, they do so with great honor and respect. My daughter, Annie, closest to Jim in age and in every other way, is almost completely adrift. She not only lost her brother, she lost her best friend. In a tragic attempt to relieve her pain, she turned to drugs.

The parallel pain of Jim's death and Annie's decline has been overwhelming. It has been a frightful awakening to learn firsthand that this world is not kind and that my children are not safe.

If I have found any catharsis through these months and years, it has been in my writing. I have chronicled Jim's illness, his death, and my journey. In the early days of Jim's battle, I wrote to maintain a website that communicated information with family and friends. The website is long gone, but I have continued to write. My writing has forced me to collide with the depths of my grief and the reality of my loss.

Thursday of this week, we will travel to Northern Minnesota, LuAnn's and my homeland, to bury Jim's cremains in our family cemetery. We will lay him next to my mom. The act of cremation postponed difficult decisions and painful ceremonies in those first dreadful days only to have to face them now. My wife is terribly distraught in anticipation. We're hoping for some kind of comfort.

We have found little comfort here in Michigan. We have no family here and very few close friends. We stopped attending church in the last months of Jim's illness because he couldn't be left alone. It's been years now and we have not returned. I don't know if we ever will. I don't know if that's right or wrong, good or bad. It's simply what we've done.

That was all I wrote. And, like I said, I never went back. Grief recovery groups aren't for everyone. Groups aren't for everyone.

MEMORIES ARE A HARD THING

Upon the burial of our beloved son.

MEMORIES ARE A HARD THING.

We stand here today with memories flooding over us. We could tell many tales of happy days, fun times, and the goodness of a life well-lived. We could recall accomplishments attained and kindnesses and generosities shown. We could even recount embarrassing moments that have now mellowed into stories that let us laugh.

But with every thought, with every memory of what once was, our hearts cry out with the reality of what will never be again.

Memories are a hard thing.

THE IMPOSSIBLE

WE HAVE BURIED THE REMAINS OF OUR BELOVED SON.
Jim's ashes now lie in the rich Minnesota soil near to where his grandmother lies and in the same plot in which some day his mother and I will lie.

Friday afternoon the boys and I dug Jim's grave. The following day we gathered.

Jim's ashes were placed in a simple wooden box made of polished walnut. Each of us held Jim in turn. Then we wrapped the box in a quilt my grandmother had made for me when I was a baby and placed it in the ground.

Then we did the impossible.

We covered it all with cold dirt.

I wanted to die.

THE SPIRITUAL DIMENSION

SUFFERING THE DEATH OF MY SON WAS LIKE PASSING
into a new dimension. I see things I never saw before, things

that others don't seem to see. It's as if my eyes, my heart, and my mind were pried opened for the first time. As if God has entrusted me with vision that only comes through great pain. Grief has given me new eyes, new ears, and a new heart. I can see things for what they are. I can hear things that didn't seem to be there before. I can feel at a depth that some don't even realize exists.

I must do something with these new senses. I must share what I see, hear, and feel. I must give warning, encouragement, and hope.

Every quest I have ever undertaken tends to reveal more of what I don't know than what I do—a newly found ignorance so to speak. The past five years of my life have been marked by the realization of how much I have yet to learn.

My firstborn son was diagnosed with an untreatable cancer. Eight months later, he was gone. He has been gone for five years. The death of my son and the suffering he endured has caused me to rethink nearly everything I have been taught about life and about God. It's like I've dumped out all the contents of an old trunk and am now attempting to repack it. Many things have slipped away as unimportant or irrelevant. Nothing gets back in easily. Every belief gets tried and tested. I refuse to believe anything "just because"—just because I used to, just because someone says I ought to, just because it's easy to, or just because I want to.

My search has led me to some new places. It has also, in many cases, brought me back to a place I've always been. It's been humbling. Dear God, it's been humbling. It would have been easier had I not started out as such a proud and arrogant man.

There remains an aching in my soul—a longing for truth. I lie awake with it. I weep and wail over it. It is this deep yearning that moves me and motivates everything I do, everything I think, and everything I write.

I have been criticized for this rethinking. It's been suggested that I've lost my faith or that I've adopted some strange spirituality. I have not lost my faith. Nothing about my spirituality has changed. It's my humanity that has changed. It's my beliefs that have changed. There is nothing unspiritual about questioning my beliefs in light of my son's death. To suffer the death of my son without questioning my beliefs— that would be wrong. That would be unspiritual. That would be inhuman.

Don't let this confuse you. My faith and my beliefs are two very separate things.

LAYER UPON LAYER

SHORTLY AFTER JIM DIED, I MET A MAN WHO HAD LOST his son. He told me it took five years before he felt a renewed sense of focus and purpose in his life. At the time, I couldn't comprehend his words, but I never forgot them. I realize now, half a decade later, that I've been comparing myself to that man and reluctantly looking forward to this five-year mark.

Looking back, I recognize that man, that father, was very different from me. His loss was similar, but his situation was not at all the same. His relationship with his son was much different than mine; he hadn't watched his son suffer; he hadn't been holding his son the moment he died. He hadn't lost his job only weeks after losing his son. He hadn't struggled for over two years to find work. His resources hadn't come unraveled. He hadn't buried his mother, his father-in-law, four uncles, an aunt, a cousin, and a dear friend in the aftermath of his loss. Though his single loss was great—the ultimate loss—he didn't indicate any additional losses. There were no additional layers to his grief.

As the years pass, I've lost track of the layers to my grief—layer upon layer upon layer. And now, as unbelievable as it seems, it's been five years. It's been five years since my beloved son slipped from my arms.

I've unwillingly anticipated this day. I hate the fact that five years have passed since I held my precious boy. Yet, I have wondered if there is something about this five-year point. I have wondered if this next year will mark the beginning of a renewed focus and purpose for me.

I have little hope of that.

It's Been Five Years: Reflections on a Reluctant Journey

No one tells you about the close connection between grief and anger. The anguish of loss breaks your heart but it also boils your blood.

WHEN JIM DIED, I FOUND THAT MY ANGER HAD NO BOUNDS. I was so angry. I was angry at God for letting my precious boy die. I was angry at myself because I was powerless to prevent his death. I was angry at Jim for dying. And I was angry at everyone else because they still lived.

In a terrifying downward spiral, my grief and loss mixed with bitterness and resentment. I wanted everyone to die. I wanted everyone else's sons to die.

I wanted to die.

It wasn't fair. If my son couldn't live, then no sons should live.

It was the inequity I despised. This shouldn't have happened to my son. This shouldn't have happened to my family. We'd had enough pain and loss. It should have been someone else's turn. This should have happened to someone else's family—someone else's son.

The darkest, most heart-stopping pain and loss of this doesn't find most people. It found me.

I was helpless. I was angry because I was helpless. I had no control. There was nothing I could do to stop my son's cancer. There was nothing I could do to prevent him from dying. I couldn't change what was happening. I have come to realize that there's nothing I can do to stop what might come to me today or hold back the tide of what may come tomorrow. Whatever illusions I had of control died with my son. I was helpless. I was angry.

I am angry still.

It's been five years.

> *No one tells you about the close connection*
> *between grief and apathy. Grief is like a black*
> *hole. It sucks everything into itself until nothing*
> *is left—not even the ability to care. Not even*
> *the ability to care whether or not you care.*

When Jim died, I went numb. Other than the searing pain of grief, I couldn't feel anything. I was aware of my lack of feeling. I *felt* the numbness. I assumed it was shock. I assumed it was some kind of protective mechanism that kept me from literally exploding. I assumed it would pass. But it didn't.

Death had stolen my life. I no longer cared whether or

not I lived. It wasn't that I wanted to die. I just had no more desire to live.

I fell into despair. No, worse than that. I fell into "dis-re-lationship" with everything and everyone. I wanted nothing from this life except for this life to be over. It was as if I began to dissolve.

I stopped taking care of myself. I stopped buckling my seat belt, eating healthy and exercising. I stopped all the positive routines of life. I gained a lot of weight. I aged fifteen years in only five. I didn't care about personal hygiene or fashion. Trimming my hair, shaving, picking out clothes that were different every day, or even clean, became tasks that were not only too demanding, but simply didn't matter. As much as I wanted to sleep, most nights I couldn't. So I didn't. And I didn't care that I didn't. I lived in a state of exhaustion, and I didn't care.

That might have been the worst of it, the fact that I just didn't care. Moreover, I didn't care that I didn't care. Languor, that indolent lethargy of body, mind, and soul, threatened my very existence. The ancients called it *acedia*. My ability to care was broken, and I didn't care that it was broken.

It's getting better, but it's still broken. I'm still broken.

It's been five years.

> *No one tells you about the close connection*
> *between grief and absence. No one tells you that*
> *the longer someone is gone, the more you miss*

them—that time doesn't heal the hurt, it just
lengthens the wound.

I didn't think I would still hurt so badly and so much of the time after five years. I didn't think that an absence of five years would still feel so fresh.

The longer my son is gone from me, the more I miss him. It's the absence I can't get used to. It's the all-inclusive, relentless absence. Jim is never coming back. I will never see him, touch him, or know him. I can't bear that thought.

Jim was twenty-four years old when he died. Nate turned twenty-four last month. Annie turned twenty-four two years ago. John will turn twenty-four in two years. Two of my children have already surpassed their brother's life. Soon they will have all outlived him. Jim will always be twenty-four years old in my heart and mind. Annie, Nate, and John will get married, have children, and grow old, but Jim will forever be a twenty-four-year-old.

Most days I can't contain the thought of his absence.

The grief over the loss of a child takes a parent to the brink of insanity. It's a dark journey from which they never entirely return, a deep wound which never completely heals. I have been out of my mind for five years. In a real sense, I have been gone too. I lost my son and then I lost myself. I miss my son and, frankly, I miss me.

I am missing still.

It's been five years.

No one tells you about the close connection between grief and abandonment. Most people, after five years, will either forget about your pain or assume that you have had sufficient time to heal—to get better, to get over it. Very few people will think to ask how you're doing or take time to encourage you.

The loss of my son brought a grief so intense and raw that most people have been unable to tolerate it on my behalf for more than a few brief moments, much less five full years. Friends and family have grown accustomed to my loss. What they fail to realize is that I have not. Certainly that initial, raw, heart-stopping pain has subsided, but my grief and the ache of Jim's absence have not lessened. Some days, without warning, I find myself overwhelmed by that early grief and that empty ache.

Unfortunately—unforgivably—the past years have been marked by words of criticism and rebuke for having not sufficiently overcome my grief. It's one thing to encounter the babbling of fools. It's another to endure the betrayal of friends. It's one thing to forgive the ignorance. It's another to forget the arrogance. The result is a feeling of abandonment and a realization that no one is ever going to comprehend my loss. Grief is lonely. No one, not even my wife, the mother of my son, has been able to fully enter into my grief—nor I into hers.

Grief is a selfish thing. People who grieve aren't selfish;

the grief itself is selfish. Grief has emptied me. My soul is a hollow void where bitter wind blows without mercy. I have never been so lonely.

I am lonely still.

It's been five years.

CHANGES

AS DIFFICULT AS THEY ARE TO SEE, THERE HAVE BEEN changes in the past five years.

One change this year was the way in which we celebrated Jim's birthday. We celebrated his final birthday, his twenty-fourth, in his hospital room, Thursday, November 10, 2005, the day before he died. We have celebrated his birthday every year since. One of Jim's final gifts to us was that he declared he would "make it to Friday." He decided he would not die on his birthday. And, true to his word and to his will, he did just that. As a result, we will always be able to celebrate his birthday remembering his life, not his death.

Every year we have made a pilgrimage to the only marker here in Michigan. That place of remembrance located at the field house of a local college where some dear friends placed a terracotta tile amongst other memorials, "In memory of Jim Sollom, our beloved son." Each year, on Jim's birthday, we have gone there to remember his wonderful life and mourn the reality of the following day. We would bring a candle, huddle in a circle, and share words of love and remembrance. Everyone would cry. I would try to pray. The first year, several of Jim's friends joined us. The next year there were not so many. The third year it was just our family. Last year, only LuAnn, John, and myself.

This year was different. This year Annie was here and Nate came home from Chicago. We were "all" together. As the evening began, Nathan took me aside and said, "Dad, I don't want to go to the field house this year. It's too cold and wet and, frankly, it's too morbid. I miss Jim all year long. Tonight I just want to be together with my family and remember the good things about life." I cried. I asked everyone what they felt, and they agreed with Nate. LuAnn cried. So, we all stayed home that night. We lit a lot of candles, burned some incense, and built a fire in the fireplace. We ate a hearty meal and spent a long evening looking at pictures and laughing. We cried some but, for the most part, we laughed.

That's a change.

My kids all love each other so much. And they all love their old mom and dad. The kids genuinely like being together and enjoy each other's company. They laugh—my goodness how they laugh. That's a really good thing. And here's an amazing thing: They have forgiven me for not being myself and for not being there for them these past five years.

I've disappointed a lot of people in the past five years. I have not been a good friend. I've had to say I am sorry for that. I have not been the husband and father my beloved wife and precious children have needed me to be. I have asked each of them for their forgiveness. I fear that I wasn't everything Jim needed me to be in the midst of his suffering. I know that Jim forgives me. (But how do I forgive myself? How does a father forgive himself for not being able to keep his son from dying?)

My children have forgiven me. I know they have because I've apologized to each of them for my weakness and my absence and they have all said they forgive me. That's a good thing.

That's a change.

There is a change in me regarding my personal care. I am thinking about my well-being this year. I am working at exercise, healthy eating, and weight loss. I am wearing brighter colored clothes and putting on a clean pair of socks every day. I still wear my hair too long for a man my age and go too many days before shaving my neck, but I keep my hair and beard clean and trimmed.

This past year, LuAnn and I have been reclaiming our empty nest. We have converted Annie's and John's rooms into guest rooms and Nate's basement room into a family room. We are systematically removing wallpaper and painting every wall in the house. I kept better care of the lawn and gardens last summer and might even get around to painting the fence and cleaning the windows this next year. Performing these chores might seem like normal, everyday things to most people. To me they've been insurmountable, but I'm actually beginning to do them.

That's a change.

LuAnn and I have changed. Our marriage has changed. We have managed to survive where many do not. The loss of a child strips away the pretense. In that intense pain, there's no room left for pretending. In that raw grief, there's not enough strength to be anybody other than who you are. It got real confusing for a while. LuAnn and I felt like we were losing touch with each other and with ourselves. What we were losing touch with was the pretense, the image, and the pretending—the pretending to be who we thought we were supposed to be. When that façade finally died, our true selves began to come through.

LuAnn and I have struggled desperately. Our mutual pain has torn gaping holes in each other's hearts. We have trampled each other's souls. It's been an unbearable journey. But, as I look back, the depth of our struggle has been matched by the depth of our love. I truly love my wife. I have found that true love doesn't always have to be a romantic love, a happy love, or a victorious love. True love is not what I expected it to be. It's a broken thing. It bleeds and aches. But it's the most honest emotion I've ever known.

That's a change. (Actually, it's more like the intense realization of something I've always known.)

There has been a change in my soul—my spirituality. I stopped attending church services about a month before Jim died. Other than a handful of feeble attempts, I haven't returned since. Nevertheless, despite the absence of conventional religion, I am becoming more aware of the constant abiding Presence of God. This aspect of change is difficult to understand and even more difficult to explain.

I'm not more aware of God because I have felt His Presence but because I have felt His absence. Driven by that sense of His absence and a feeling of abandonment, I have sought Him with all my might.

I'm learning there's a huge difference between faith and confidence. I'm coming to a place where I no longer need God to prove Himself or expose Himself. God is with me. He always has been and always will be. He won't disappear when I'm broken or sad. He won't leave me when I misbehave or act badly.

I'm discovering more substantial, tried-and-true definitions for things like faith, mercy, love, and grace—a grace that only makes sense when it comes from a context of real, bitter, inconsolable pain. I'm coming to understand that genuine mercy doesn't necessarily make me feel better. Understand that when the Bible says I can have "peace that passes understanding" it means exactly that—peace that I can't understand. (On most days, however, I'd settle for a little peace I could understand.)

I pray constantly, but the romance is gone. There is no more poetry in my prayer, no more clever phrases or religious rhetoric. I don't pray out loud much anymore—in public, or at meals. Yet, even though my prayers consist of little more than, "Oh God, Oh God, Oh God," accompanied by deep sighs and groaning, they never cease. There is an intense intimacy in that. To know God in deep, deep sorrow is so entirely different than knowing Him in joy.

I've come to know God as a Father—an identity that took on new meaning and a new solidarity with God as I watched my son die. I've come to know myself as a beloved son of God—the God and Father of all. I have come to know the father-heart of God even as I have come to know my own father-heart.

The loss of my son changed my heart. It's a gentler heart now—kinder, wiser perhaps. The loss of my son deepened my heart, softened it, but utterly broke it. My heart is still broken. It always will be. It will never be restored. But it's whole. I don't understand that. There is a new "wholeness" about me, yet the brokenness remains. I think it has something to do with seeing my heart, not as broken apart but as broken open. Broken apart, my heart fell away from me—from life and from the lives of those around me—in shattered pieces that lost all sense of place and purpose. Broken open, my heart lies exposed and undefended, allowing life—my life and all living things—to fall into it and be, somehow, surrounded by it. Embraced by it. That's grace. That's an awful grace.

But that's a change.

Some Things Never Change

PEOPLE TELL ME I'VE CHANGED. A FEW SAY I'VE "COME A long way." What does it mean to "come a long way"? Have I come a long way *from* something or *toward* something? I don't usually ask them what they mean by that. Perhaps I don't believe it's true. Or perhaps I know a lot of what they see is just smoke and mirrors. I've learned to only let people see what they want or need to see.

Many things have not changed. Some will never change.

The holidays are here, and Jim will still not be joining us. Thanksgiving has just passed. There was still an empty chair at our table. As LuAnn and I spent Thanksgiving morning preparing the kids' favorite foods, we became overwhelmed and had to take a moment to ourselves. We sat together in my chair, held each other tightly, and had ourselves a good long cry. We are still overcome by the pain, and we still get lost in our grief.

That will never change.

I wouldn't want it to.

THE SACRED PAINTING: A STORY OF REDEMPTION

ONE OF JIM'S CLOSEST FRIENDS IS A GIFTED ARTIST. IN an attempt to process his grief, this young man chose a snapshot, taken of Jim as he lay dying in his hospital bed, and turned it into a large oil painting. It was on a huge canvas, measuring three by five feet. It was painted in dark shadows and presented with dramatic, violent strokes. Even as he was painting, I understood why this young man needed to capture the intense suffering of his friend, but I remember wishing he wasn't.

LuAnn never wanted to see the finished painting. I didn't want to either, but it was important for Jim's friend to show it to me. So, I viewed it. The image was so tragic—so morbid and gruesome. I was careful to keep it from LuAnn. She never had to see it. I wish I never had. That image haunted me for a long time, but I eventually put it out of my mind.

That changed today. LuAnn and I were making our rounds to the local second-hand stores, hoping to find winter jackets. To our horror, in the middle of an ill-kept second-hand store—leaning carelessly against all the other unwanted and forgotten pictures—was that terrifying painting of our dying son.

At first LuAnn didn't see it. She saw me and asked what was wrong. I had turned white and was frightening her.

Then she saw it, the painting she had never seen. The painting she had never wanted to see, the painting I had tried so hard to keep her from seeing.

We stood together in utter shock. I couldn't breathe. My heart pounded in my chest. My mind couldn't process what I was seeing. Why was that dreadful image there? How could that have happened? What terrible progression of events could have brought that intensely personal painting to such a poor and lowly public display? Why would anyone do that to our precious son?

I found an attendant, told her who the young man was, and asked if I could please take the painting away. She said she couldn't give it to me. I would have to buy it. She also said, as some kind of consolation, that she would be willing to put it aside. Put it aside? She would "put it aside"? It had already been "put aside." I couldn't believe what was happening. I told her I couldn't let her keep it. I couldn't let her put it aside, or even let it stay there. I couldn't let anyone do that to my son ever again.

I purchased the painting, loaded it in our van, and took it home.

I wished I hadn't seen it there, lying on that dirty, second-hand floor, where clumsy feet could kick it and grubby hands could touch it. I wished I hadn't learned what had become of that painting. Yet, amidst my anger and shock I was glad I had found it—relieved that I had rescued it, redeemed it. I had saved not only my son's memory, but his dignity. I am still torn to the core of my soul by what we've just suffered, but now I can deal with that picture myself.

Everyone is forgetting my son. No one wants to remember. For some, it's as if my dear boy never existed. For some, he's nothing more than a discarded painting collecting dust at a second-hand store. There are people out there careless enough to do that to my son. It makes me so sad. That sadness will only get worse as the years go by. Everyone will continue to forget. I can't think of a more wretched reminder of that than what LuAnn and I just endured.

As LuAnn and I transported that terrifying painting back to our home, I had no idea what we would do with it—what would come of it. We couldn't keep it. We couldn't bear that. I couldn't destroy it. How could I bring myself to do that? I stowed it away in a safe and out-of-sight place, believing an idea would come—some inspiration would reveal my next step.

The inspiration came the very next day: Paint another painting over it. Cover that dark death with color and life—brightness and light. My family and I would always know what lies just beneath the surface, but the rest of the world would not.

The painting had been done with a very thick layer of

paint. I knew I would have to find an artist who painted with equal intensity. I thought of Joel Tanis, an accomplished artist who specializes in paintings with childlike beauty and lots of color and light—and lots of paint.

I sent Joel a copy of this Sacred Painting story. I also sent him a copy of the original photos of Jim in his hospital bed and a photo of the "rescued" painting.

A few days later, I met with Joel. I brought the huge canvas. He heard the story again. He saw the actual painting. He wept. I knew at that moment I had chosen the right artist. His tenderness was touching and affirming.

The working title of the painting is *Redemption.*

The painting is done. I picked it up and brought it home. It feels good to have it finished. I'm glad to have it home. The kids and LuAnn have seen it. We are all so pleased and relieved.

Joel has painted a bright and beautiful mountain scene. He took his inspiration from a photo I gave him of Jim and his sister in the San Bernardino Mountains. We lived there in the 1990s.

Much of the substance and many of the lines remain from the original painting—the flow, the strokes, and even some colors. The painting of our Jim on his deathbed literally contained the direction and shape of the resulting mountain scene.

One of Joel's trademarks, especially with his children's

paintings, is to include words—verses and sayings that blend into the picture and enhance the message. These beautiful words from Frederick Buechner, in subtle and wispy lines, graced the sky in our Jim's Sacred Painting:

> *At certain rare moments of greenness and stillness, we are shepherded by the knowledge that, though all is far from right with the world you and I know anything about, all is right deep down. All will be right at last.*

It is all such a treasure—a terrible and wonderful treasure.

DON'T STOP TRYING

THERE'S A DIFFERENCE BETWEEN HAVING EMPATHY FOR someone and being grateful you're not them. A difference between caring about someone and feeling sorry for them. There is a world of difference between compassion and pity. The problem is, we use them interchangeably and call them both *compassion*. To have genuine care and compassion for someone, to join with the sorrow and plunge deeply into the suffering of another, might not even be possible. I'm not sure I've ever done it, and I'm a pretty sensitive guy.

People try. I try. I think, to a degree, we all try. We just can't do it. We can't really enter into another's life.

Our lives are too busy. We just don't have the time and energy for other people's trouble. We all have enough trouble of our own. None of us is to blame. We simply cannot enter into another's skin. We can't even walk in someone else's shoes, as much as we say we can. We romanticize that notion.

We're alone. Inside ourselves, we're alone. We all know that. But maybe knowing that isn't so bad. Maybe the consolation is that *we're all alone together*. Maybe knowing what we can't do for each other allows us to do what we can. If we stop expecting things to be what they're not, they can start being what they are.

LuAnn and I have been in love since we were fifteen years old. We know each other like no one else. We love each other like no one else. But even we have been incapable of comforting each other. We come close. Closer than anyone else. But we fall short of making the difference we truly wish we could make.

If I can't make a difference in LuAnn's pain, how can I make a difference in anyone else's? Why would anyone think they could make a difference in mine?

But don't stop trying. Let's none of us ever stop trying. I'm tired of the old adages that say there is no such thing as *trying*—that there is only *doing* or *not doing*. It's clever, but it's not true. Most days, all we have is trying.

No Logic in Grief

LuAnn AND I SPENT MOST OF TODAY AT A STATE PARK that borders Lake Michigan. It's been six years today since Jim died.

We traversed the dunes for several miles. A portion of that was along the sandy beach. The wind was strong and cold as it blew in off the water. The water was rough and wild and in nearly as much turmoil as my troubled soul. Jim loved the lake—loved her dearly.

As LuAnn and I walked across the blowing sand, the emotional trauma of the day and the relentless waves overwhelmed me. I began to cry. I walked and cried, hidden from LuAnn's eyes by the hood she wore for protection from the wind and hidden from her ears by the sound of the crashing waves. Soon my crying turned to weeping and I could no longer sustain my walk or restrain my emotion. I leaned on my hiking sticks and sobbed. My beloved came to my side and we wept together—wept and wailed. There was no more control. The exhaustion besieged me. I screamed out against the thundering sea and the helplessness of it all. Like a man insane, I ran to the water's edge, kicking at the waves and defying their power.

"I defy your power!" I cried. "My boy loved you, and you did nothing to save him!"

There was no sense in my words, no rationale in my actions. There is no logic in grief.

I stood there, my pants drenched by the waves and my boots filled with icy water. I wept again. Only this time my weeping was different. There was something different in the water.

Jim was in the water.

I no longer saw the waves as taunting me. I saw Jim in the waves. I saw my brave, strong boy wrestling with that great watery love of his life—wrestling with all his might—reaching out to touch his mother and me. I welcomed the water. It no longer felt cold. I bent over, lowered my hands into the sand, and caressed the next wave that reached me.

I returned to LuAnn, and we wept again. It seemed like the waves lessened then.

After a few moments, we turned to go. As we did, it was as if we were releasing our precious Jim to the place he loved so much. We returned to the wooded path and sat at the first bench we encountered. We were completely drained—exhausted by our encounter.

We rested.

What Happened to the Insanity?

FOR MANY YEARS, NOTHING HAS MADE MUCH SENSE. My life has been in ruins, my mind has been a jumble. I've stood on the brink, on the edge of confusion and despair, and wondered why I don't just jump. I've been insane. I've questioned everything and everyone—myself included. I've wrestled with my life, with God, and with every word I've written. Last night, as I wrote, everything seemed too easy, too calm, and too predictable. There was no wrestling. My reasoning was sound and my assertions palatable. My tone was that of one who had given up the fight and relinquished the struggle. My words had the ring of someone who had settled for the easy way out—someone who had opted for a lie.

What happened to the insanity?

I know my problem. I'm afraid. Someone might read this. Maybe a lot of someones. My family and friends might read this. I can't come off as insane. That would be…well, insane. I need to "get it together." I need to package this neatly, input some appropriate proof texts, and pull together some intelligent, if not impressive, answers to the "problems" of pain, loss, grief, and brokenness.

What am I afraid of? Criticism? Rejection? Not getting the words right? Why should I be afraid? For the past seven years, my own life has terrified me. Why should the telling of it be any more frightful?

What happened to the struggle?

This shouldn't be easy. It hasn't been easy yet, not even once. I can't sit by with idle complacency and let it get easy now.

I know my problem. I'm pretending to be a writer. I'm working so hard at getting all the words right that I'm getting them all wrong. They're too slick and polished. They're too *careful*, too *crafted*, and too *calculated*. *My efforts are dripping with the sweet and savory syrup of well-chosen rhetorical prose.* My words run the risk of becoming just like those last two sentences—sappy sentimentality dripping with overly applied alliteration. I can do sappy. I can overuse alliteration.

Dear God, save me from that.

What's the matter with me? Snap out of it. Who am I trying to impress?

I don't have to be perfect. In fact, I shouldn't be. Perfect words for an imperfect world, where's the sense in that? That wouldn't be true. Above all, I long to be true—true to myself, true to my story, and true to the truth about brokenness. Perfection probably won't come into play.

Truth is a vulnerable and dangerous thing. Truth divides.

239

Some people who read the truths in my writing might look away in objection and disfavor when they meet me on the street. Others will stop and shake my hand and won't be able to stop shaking it until they have said, "Finally, finally, finally" enough times to confess their reality and convince me just how long they have waited for someone to tell the truth—their truth.

Acknowledging someone else's truth is difficult for some, impossible for others. I will have to live with that.

Let the insanity begin…again.

NOT ANYMORE

HARD TIMES, IF THEY DON'T RUN YOU AGROUND, BECOME the heavy ballast buried deep in the keel of your ship that helps you hold a steady course through even deeper and rougher waters.

A lot of weight has settled deep down in the
bones of this old boat.

Some days it pulls me so low, I swear I'm scraping bottom, afraid I'll tear up my hull on the jagged rocks. How can a craft be pulled down so low and still stay afloat?

Hard times came to me like a merciless torrent of tidal waves beating upon what had always seemed like a safe and stable ship. My life became more than I could handle. I was drowning, sinking into a dark abyss.

Unbearable events and unthinkable consequences heaped upon me—layer upon layer upon layer. The storms of life came to my door, and I could not prevail. The brokenness and heartache of grief and loss overwhelmed me. I could not endure the sheer dailiness of my own existence.

My hard times have settled deep into my life to stabilize me when the storms of life threaten to destroy. That ballast will allow me to navigate the even more treacherous waters that lie ahead. That ballast will also help maneuver those waters on behalf of others.

The hard times will come again. Of course they will. It is the nature and the rhythm of this life. But the waves will not overcome me. I will not capsize. Not this time. Not today.

Not anymore.

The waves may beat upon my hull and flood my decks, but I will remain afloat. I will not go down. Not again.

Not anymore.

There was a day when the slightest wind threw me off course, but not today.

Not anymore.

There was a day when the smallest wave would thrash me upon the rocks, but not today.

Not anymore.

AT THE BOTTOM OF THE ABYSS

LIFE DOES NOT CARRY A MORE OVERWHELMING LOSS than the death of a child. My grief and pain have been terrible things. Yet, something is beginning to happen. After all these years—after all these dreadful days and sleepless nights—something is stirring.

I don't understand exactly what it is. It's a kind of "knowing." An awareness and a mindfulness. It's a realization. An intention.

I have known hard times. I have stood at the edge of an unfathomable abyss and stared into its absolute darkness—its absence of light. I have known the deep anguish of being utterly abandoned. Yet, as I have leaned into the abyss and felt its despair overwhelm me, I have known something else. Without understanding why or how, I have known this one thing: There's "not nothing" at the bottom.

Take heart, all who wander—at the end of all things, there is "not nothing."

THE SPIRAL OF GRIEF

THERE IS NOTHING LINEAR ABOUT GRIEF. IT ISN'T A STEP-by-step process that systematically guides you through it and eventually leads you out of it. It's more like a circle where you go around and around and around, revisiting the same feelings over and over and over again. At some point, you realize it's not so much a circle as it is a spiral. The question is whether the spiral is going up or down.

Left alone, the spiral of grief will take you down into bitterness and despair. But with a little mindfulness—just a little—you find that the spiral is working its way ever upward. Most of the movement is indistinguishable. Most of it is outside of your control and apart from any strategy or intention.

There are hidden forces working for your good.

Some call it grace. Some even come to call it mercy. I haven't decided yet what to call it. But it's there. There is always something there.

Worshiping with Pain

Without any kind of strategy, I have attended a variety of church services in the past several years. I am seeking to be in the presence of fellow believers, to confirm the resurrection of Jesus Christ, and proclaim in a weak but certain voice, God's love for all creation.

What I find feels shallow, silly, incomplete, and out of touch with the present realities of my life. So, I still don't go. I remain de-churched.

It's winter in Michigan as I write. Our doors and windows are closed tightly to block out the winter winds. Many of the churches I have attended seem like that—sealed up tight so no chill can penetrate. There seems to be the assumption that the Christian soul must live only and always in the "warmth" of God. The doors and windows of our hearts must be tightly sealed so as not to let the "wintry winds" reveal the struggle in which we actually live. There is no place for the icy sting of loss or the cold reality of grief. I suspect this practice follows the belief that the message of pain won't fill pews. Words and music that allow for, or even encourage, suffering would be far too depressing for today's happy churchgoers.

As I read the scriptures, however, I come across countless

words of lament. It's tragic if none of these sorrowful strains can be allowed to find their way into our worship. Someday I'd like to enter a church and read banners hanging from the rafters that declare:

> "We will only move as fast as our slowest runner."
>
> "We will only wade in as deep as our poorest swimmer."
>
> "We will only be as whole as our most broken heart."
>
> "We will only be as happy as our saddest child."
>
> "We will only be a strong as our weakest link."

Instead I encounter the typical churchy slogans: "Our God Reigns." "Rejoice in the Lord." "God is Good." I'm asked to stand and clap and sing, to greet my neighbor with a smile and shout "Halleluiah!" I'm asked to repeat romanticized lyrics about how lovely and wonderful He is. It makes me want to shout, instead, about how ruthless and merciless He is.

I realize I'm being critical and I'm picking away at the small things. Maybe there's more hope if I can focus on a larger perspective. If my life is about something greater than me—other than me—then maybe I don't have to understand every little thing that happens. If my son's death is about something bigger than him or me, then maybe I don't have to make sense of it—make up a reason for it.

Maybe I don't have to understand everything. Maybe I

don't have to act like I know what I'm doing, or pretend I'm happy and content, or stand up and clap every time I sing.

Maybe I don't have to sing.

GOD'S PRESENCE CAN BE AS FRIGHTENING AS HIS ABSENCE

I WON'T SAY THAT THIS SEASON HAS GOTTEN ANY easier or that this day—this Christmas Eve day—is not still one of the more difficult ones for me. We had a nice snowfall overnight. Fluffy cotton clings to absolutely everything. We have a perfectly picturesque white Christmas. And the sun is shining. That helps.

I hope to bring some sense of festivity to our home today. We don't decorate like we used to. We just got our tree yesterday and will put it up tonight.

I'll spend today wrapping presents, cleaning house, and baking. LuAnn has locked herself in her office and work today. Annie also works today, and John works tomorrow, but we will all be together tonight. Nathan will be with a friend's family in the Seattle area. He's encountered some hard times this fall, and he's feeling alone and broken. His young wife met someone online and left our dear boy.

I am fast approaching a place where the joys of parenthood will no longer outweigh the sorrows. (I can't believe I said that, but I think it's true.)

Nathan's new pain could easily reinforce his belief that God is impotent to hold back the tide of grief and loss and that the reality of Jesus Christ, even at this season of the year, is no reality at all.

I confess that in my own experience, the reality of Christ ebbs and flows—sometimes on a moment-by-moment basis. I have found, as have many, that the reality of Christ is most often heightened in times of trouble and brokenness. It's no wonder we come to equate the reality of Christ with fear and trembling. Drawing near to God can, indeed, be frightening. If we could even begin to comprehend the immense fierceness of God, we would think twice before approaching that kind of ferocity.

We dare not claim a God who is unapproachable, so we have "dummied" Him down. We have made Christ so familiar, that He has become unimportant; so common that He has become insignificant; so friendly that we no longer fear Him. We have required that "drawing near to God" results in comfort rather than conflict. And I have said before, even an act like "being crucified with Christ" has been romanticized. In a life of surrender to God, we may come to a place of acceptance and trust, where we decide to receive all these trials into our lives, but none of us could say we actually desire them. Why God chose an economy of growth that would be enhanced by trials, I'll never know. It would be easier to "sell" a Gospel that was filled with a little more abundance and a little less abandonment.

Even today, as we celebrate the God who came to be "with us," I still feel the ache of His absence—even now, after all these years.

LEAVING CLARITY BEHIND

As I come to the close of another year, I find myself thinking and writing and wrestling with God over all that has befallen me in my life. I battle the inequity of it all and fight against bitterness and despair. I fear that my words, an honest expression of my heart, may still, after all these years, sound uncertain and unclear.

I have spent my life in devotion to God and longed to surrender and sacrifice to Him everything that I hold dear. I have stood willing to give up everything to follow God. I never dreamed that the health and well-being and the very life of my children would be the things He would take from me.

Twenty years agob, I lost my singing voice and my music career to calcified nodules and a damaged larynx. God took my song. I thought His logic was skewed. Why take away that? Why take from me what I thought was the best gift He'd given me by which to serve Him? Why take away what I thought I had already given Him? Now, with the great gifts of my children being taken from me, I *know* there is no logic to God's actions, and it has left me undone...again.

There is no logic with which to explain the past or with which to anticipate the future. Leaving things like logic and clarity behind might be the only way to endure the brokenness of this world. You'll have to trust me on this even as I have chosen to trust God. Which I have...and do.

Which is not logical.

Life Has Changed

For most of us, the first half of life brings a time of abundance—a time when everything is new. More is given to us than is taken away. Then somewhere along the way, we cross an invisible line and all that changes. The second half of life becomes a time of scarcity—a time when everything turns old. As time passes, more and more is taken from us. It is the natural way of life. It's the backside of the circle of life. We all cross that line. Some cross it before others.

My life has changed. It changed the day my child was taken from me. Nothing will ever be the same. I have crossed that invisible line—a threshold that has permanently separated me from the man I once was.

I have met many parents whose children have died. Their lives have been forever changed. Life as they knew it ended. I have yet to meet a "surviving" parent for whom that is not true. Those who deny it eventually realize they have been deceiving themselves.

I didn't ask for this change—this comprehension. I won't impose it upon another. It's better for them that they do not understand. I would rather I did not bear this comprehension myself. I know things I wish I didn't know—things I wish I could un-know. But I can't.

All the positive thinking, behavioral modification, developmental psychology, transformational education, lifestyle enrichments, and personal makeovers won't bring my son back or mend the broken heart that bleeds in my chest. There are things that come to us in this life that simply cannot be fixed. There are broken things in the world that will always be broken. The world, as we know it, is broken. Life, as we know it, is broken. Those who have claimed the opposite have preached a false Gospel, peddled a false hope, and sabotaged my journey.

However, I am starting to wonder if there's something more rising up from the depths. As damnable as all this has been, and as much as I would give anything and everything to have my son back in my arms, something life-giving is growing out of the ashes—something that would not have grown without that all-consuming fire.

I will never say that I am thankful to God for my son's death—that his pain and suffering were some twisted form of disguised grace. Never. That would be an atrocity. I will, however, acknowledge that God can, and has, and always will take something that is evil and bring something good of it—that He can and will breathe new life into my dry bones. Given enough time and enough mindfulness and enough surrender, God can redeem even the worst this life has to give.

WHAT KIND OF GOD

all I've ever wanted
for as long as I can remember
is all I will ever want
    to know God
    whatever that might require of me
    to serve God
    whatever that might take from me
        and in doing so
            in serving and knowing
    come to love God
    whatever that might mean to me
so how is it that all this
this pain and loss
has come to me

was God not

vigilant

what kind of God

repays such devotion

with such despair

the same God I know

and serve

and yes…love

COMING UP ON ANOTHER LIFE

LUANN AND I HAVE LIVED FOUR DIFFERENT LIVES.

That's not a surprising statement for people of our age. It's easy to look back and feel a degree of displacement from various *seasons of life*. What makes that reality unusual for LuAnn and me is that each life has been fifteen years in length—almost exactly.

Each "life" has had its own unique character and identity. Each held different locations—different towns, different states, even different countries. Each had distinct vocations. Each one had its own joys and sorrows. And, even more interesting, each one took a dramatic turn at the halfway mark—after six to eight years. The midway point of each fifteen-year life held a significant event. The direction of each life changed at that halfway point and seemed to always hinge on those significant events. Most often, those events were tragedies and deep losses.

LuAnn and I were born in 1954. It's now 2014. This year is the beginning of *Life Number Five*. Both LuAnn and I turn sixty this year. If we can hang in there until we're seventy-five (which we intend to), we will complete yet another grand adventure—another fifteen-year life. A whole new journey awaits us—a new story.

As frustrating and unsettling as life feels at the moment, we comfort ourselves with the notion that we are right on schedule. We are still winding down life number four, tying up loose ends and saying good-bye to who we've been for the past decade and a half. We are still making plans for our new beginning, still plotting our transition and designing our new life.

More and more, the hope of what lies ahead makes me want to get up in the morning. I have faith that a new day is coming, if for no other reason than the night has been as dark as I could have ever imagined it being.

Could the night have gotten any darker? I suppose it could have. I could have lost my voice entirely. Annie could have died. The boys could have cut us off for any number of reasons. LuAnn and I could have fallen victim to the overwhelming statistics and dissolved our marriage as a result of all the pain and loss. Unfortunately, "It could have been worse" has been little comfort when everything got as bad as it did.

This last life—the past fifteen years—feels like a lost life. Torn apart and riddled through with desperation, it's difficult for LuAnn and me to recall those years with any accuracy or fondness. Nothing moved upward. There were no visible improvements or advancements. It was a season of drastic decline. We suffered decline in the health and well-being of every aspect of our lives—physically, emotionally, socially, professionally, financially, and spiritually. We came so close to giving up, so close to believing our lives were over.

Our lives will never be what they were or even what they could have been. I will never be able to look back on my life and say everything is as it *should* be. Nothing will ever seem *right* again. Nevertheless, I can look at today with acceptance and say everything *is as it is*. I can look to the future with trust and say everything *can be good deep down*.

Acceptance and trust are good things. They are hard things, but they are good things.

Seeing Through A Father's Eyes

ANNIE HATED SHOTS, LIKE ALL KIDS DO WHEN THEY'RE

little. With a sixth sense, she could see them coming and fought all the way from home to the hospital. Absolutely nothing consoled her, but it had to be done. It was for her care and protection. All I could do was hold her down, get it over with, and get her out. I'm a big man—a big dad. My long arms could encompass her whole body. One firm clench could momentarily immobilize her. That became the routine until all her childhood vaccinations were complete.

Her daddy's strong embrace, which at any other time would have felt like a loving, full-body hug, must have felt like betrayal and violation. My firm grip, which at any other time would have felt like safety and protection, must have felt like fear and punishment.

My little girl couldn't see the situation through her father's eyes. She had no way of knowing that my breaking heart loved her more at that moment than at any other. She couldn't see that if there was any other way to prepare her with the vaccines that would prevent her from contracting deadly diseases, I would have chosen it.

My precious daughter had no way of seeing through her father's eyes.

Neither do I.

THE CRY OF MY HEART

THERE ARE THINGS I WANT TO DO IN THIS LIFE—MUST DO, long to do. I need to make a difference. I need it to matter that I lived. I want to create, contribute, and connect. I want to influence and inspire. I long to see places I've never seen, do things I've never done, and become someone I've never been.

I want to live again.

I yearn to enter into and fully engage every remaining moment of my life. I wish to wrap myself around the pain of this world and intertwine my life and my story with the stories and lives of those who inhabit this world with me. I want to rewrap all the trials and traumas I have endured and give them back to this life as my unique gift.

I want to laugh again.

Not a frivolous, forced laughter that serves to only temporarily release the pressure-cooker of anxiety that modern society and empty pleasures impose upon us, but an easy, authentic laughter born out of a place of deep peace and true joy and the ever-abiding Presence of the One who is the author of laughter.

I want to love again.

I desire to woo my wife into a final-season-of-life romance that will cause her to think she has fallen in love with me for the very first time.

I want to lose myself.

I long to submit to the deepest and broadest sensualities of the human experience and surrender control to the highest and grandest expressions of the spiritual reality—the only reality that will endure—God, Christ, and Holy Spirit, in all their fullness and mystery, alive and wildly inhabiting every fiber of my being.

This is my life, and this is the cry of my heart.

Before You Finish

This is the conclusion. I didn't call it the conclusion because I don't want you to think that anything is done—concluded. I wrote an introduction too, but I didn't call it an introduction. I called it *Before You Begin*. If I called it an introduction, I thought too many people might not read it. A lot of people don't read introductions. I read introductions, unless they're too long. That's why the introduction was short. So is the conclusion.

I often read the conclusion of a book before I start the book—even before I read the introduction. If that's what you're doing, I want you to know, it's okay. You have my permission.

If you want to know a secret, I wrote the conclusion before I wrote the book. I even wrote it before the introduction. When I first wrote it, I called it *Giving Pain a Voice*. I leave it with you as a personal letter of encouragement and hope.

> *Dear Friend,*
>
> *If in some small way my words have helped you, then they are your words too—ponder them, use them, say them, share them. If there*

is one thing that the human race has in common—that binds us together—it's grief. If my words can give voice to your grief, then scream them out at the top of your lungs or whisper them in the silence of your heart. I give them to you gladly, though at a terrible cost.

Take my words. If they benefit, embrace them. If not, discard them. In the end, they are only words. If they don't speak the language of your heart or reach into your soul, then they are only noise.

I hope what you take away from this is the realization that you are not alone. I hope I have given a voice to what you have been feeling so you can speak your pain and loss and begin to find peace.

I trust that you believe now that your grief_ is not a curse. Nor is it a blessing. It is simply where you meet God.

May the Lord bless you and keep you. May the Lord bless and keep us all.

Love,

Mike

To Connect with Mike, visit

https://mikesollom.com/

where you can sign up for his newsletter, read his blog, and learn more about him, LuAnn, and their travels through life.

15318006R00143